OIL AND NATURAL GAS

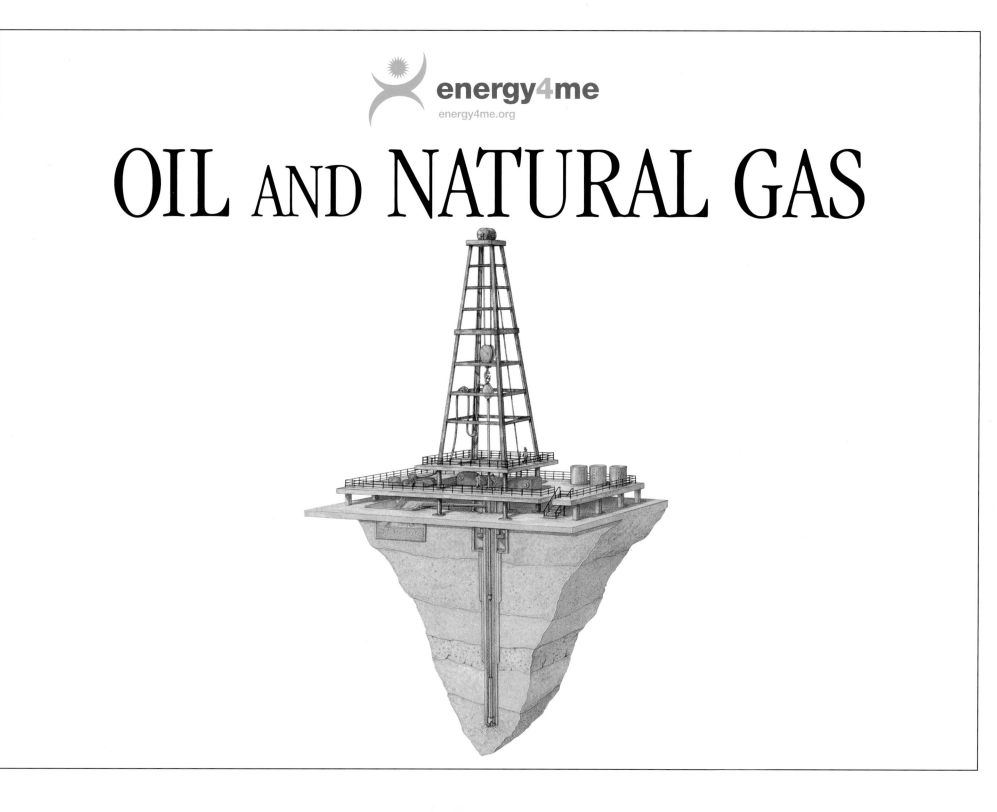

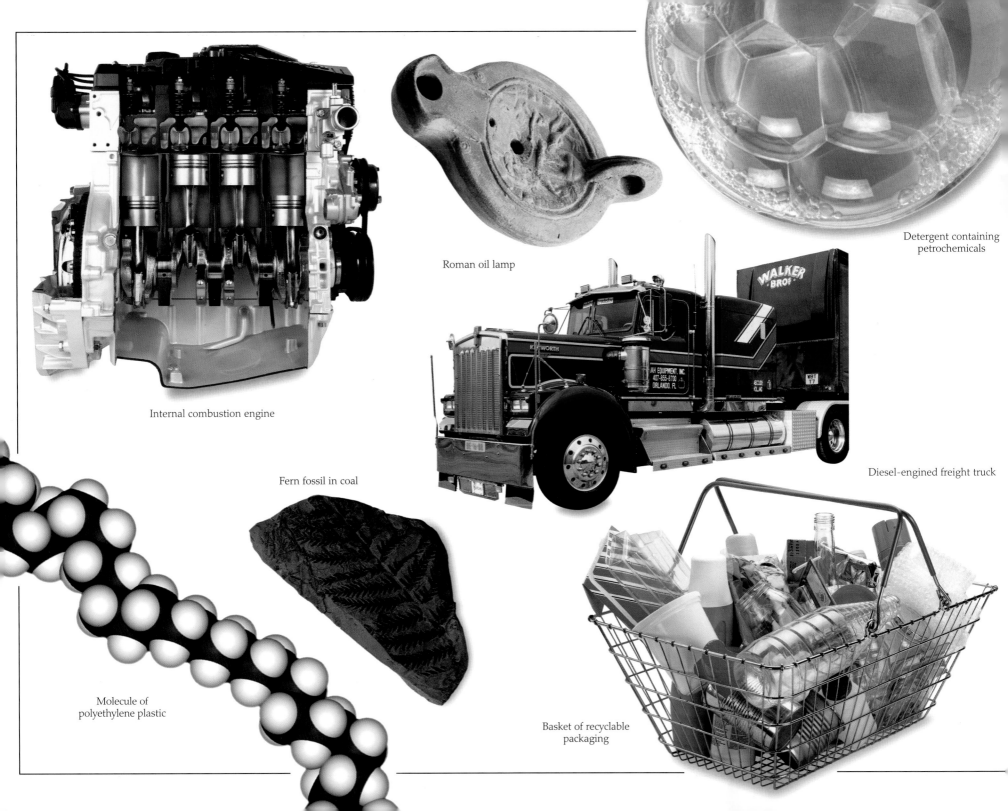

Detergent containing petrochemicals

Roman oil lamp

Internal combustion engine

Diesel-engined freight truck

Fern fossil in coal

Molecule of polyethylene plastic

Basket of recyclable packaging

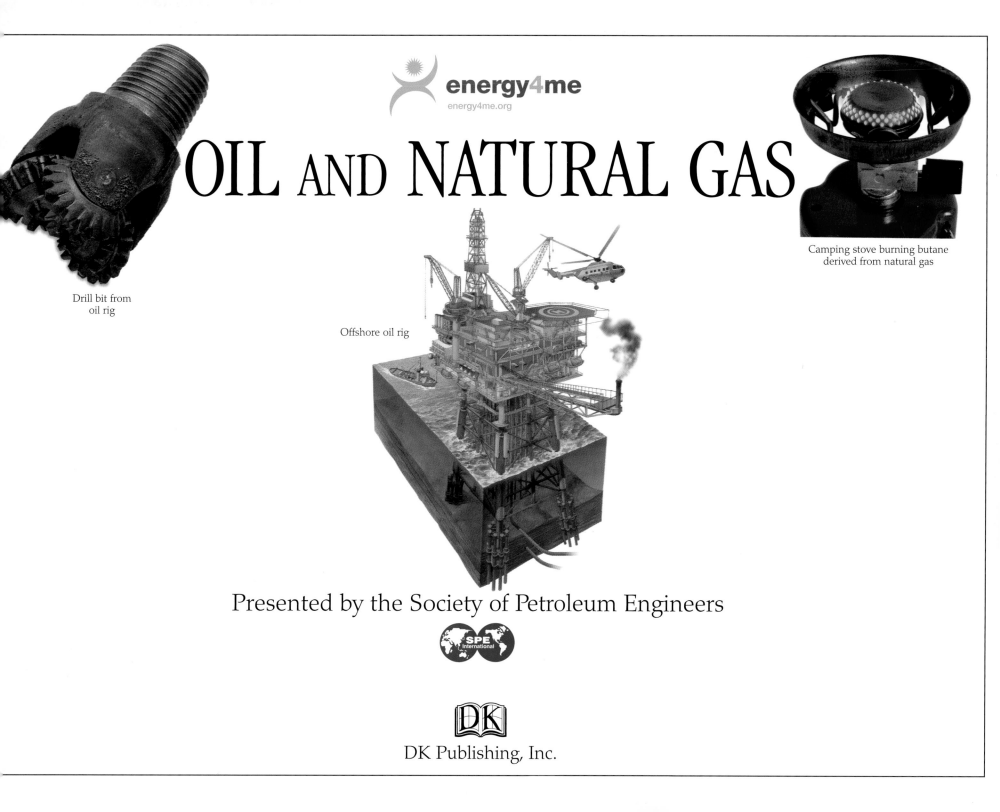

energy4me
energy4me.org

OIL AND NATURAL GAS

Drill bit from
oil rig

Camping stove burning butane
derived from natural gas

Offshore oil rig

Presented by the Society of Petroleum Engineers

SPE
International

DK

DK Publishing, Inc.

Kerosene lamp

**LONDON, NEW YORK,
MELBOURNE, MUNICH, AND DELHI**

Consultant Mike Graul

Managing editor Camilla Hallinan
Managing art editor Martin Wilson
Publishing manager Sunita Gahir
Category publisher Andrea Pinnington
DK picture library Claire Bowers
Production Georgina Hayworth
DTP designers Andy Hilliard, Siu Ho, Ben Hung
Jacket designer Andy Smith

For Cooling Brown Ltd.:
Creative director Arthur Brown
Project editor Steve Setford
Art editor Tish Jones
Picture researcher Louise Thomas

For DK New York:
Project editor Karen Whitehouse
Design and production Kelly Maish
Images Katherine Linder

First published in the United States in 2007
by DK Publishing, 375 Hudson Street,
New York, New York 10014

07 08 09 10 11 10 9 8 7 6 5 4 3 2 1
ED495 04/07

DK books are available at special discounts when purchased in
bulk for sales promotions, premiums, fundraising, or educational use.
For details, contact:
DK Publishing Special Markets
375 Hudson Street, New York, New York 10014
SpecialSales@dk.com

A catalog record for this book is available
from the Library of Congress.

ISBN: 978-0-75663-879-5

Printed in Mexico

Discover more at
www.dk.com

Plastic
ducks

Oil floating
on water

Magazines printed with
oil-based inks

Contents

Seismic survey truck

King oil

OUR WORLD IS RULED BY OIL. People have used oil for thousands of years, but in the last century we have begun to consume it in vast quantities. Daily oil consumption in the US, for example, rose from a few tens of thousands of barrels in 1900 to over 21 million barrels in 2000—more than 870 million gallons (3.3 billion liters) per day. Oil is our most important energy source, providing fuel to keep transportation going, and natural gas is used to generate the electricity on which our modern lifestyles rely. Oil is also a raw material from which many key substances, including most plastics, are made.

SUPERMARKET SECRETS
People in the world's developed countries eat a wider variety of food than ever before—thanks largely to oil. Oil fuels the planes, ships, and trucks that bring food to local stores from all around the world. It also fuels the cars in which we drive to the supermarket. And it provides the plastic packaging and the energy for the refrigeration that keep the food fresh.

LIQUID ENERGY
Unprocessed liquid oil—called crude oil—is not an impressive sight, but it is a very concentrated form of energy. In fact, there is enough energy in one barrel (42 gallons/ 159 liters) of crude oil to boil about 700 gallons (2,700 liters) of water.

Tough polycarbonate case protects delicate electronics inside

Large tankers carry 4,000–8,000 gallons (15,000–30,000 liters) or more of oil

OIL IN THE INFORMATION AGE
A sleek, slimline laptop computer looks a million miles away from crude oil, and yet without oil it could not exist. Oil not only provides the basic raw material for the polycarbonate plastic from which a computer's case is typically made, but it also provides the energy to make most of its internal parts. Oil may even have generated the electricity used to charge the computer's batteries.

FREEDOM TO TRAVEL
Gas produced from crude oil powers the cars that enable us to travel around with an ease and speed undreamed of in earlier times. Many commuters drive to work over distances that once took days to cover on horseback. But with over 600 million motor vehicles on the world's roads, and the figure rising daily, the amount of oil burned to achieve this mobility is truly staggering—about a billion barrels each month.

SLICK JUMPING

Oil plays a part even in the simplest and most basic activities. Skateboarding, for example, only really took off with the development of wheels made from an oil-based plastic called polyurethane, which is both tough and smooth. But the oil connection does not end there. Another plastic called expanded polystyrene, or EPS, provides a solid foam for a boarder's helmet. EPS squashes easily to absorb the impact from a fall. A third oil-based plastic, HDPE, is used to make knee and elbow protectors.

Impact-absorbing EPS helmet

Aluminum tank

Dense HDPE knee protector

Smooth, durable polyurethane wheels

NONSTOP CITIES

Seen from space at night, the world's cities twinkle in the darkness like stars in the sky. The brightness of our cities is only achieved by consuming a huge amount of energy—and much of this is obtained from oil. All this light not only makes cities safer, but it allows essential activities to go on right through the night.

Satellite view of Asia at night

Wheat

OIL ON THE FARM

Farming in the developed world has been transformed by oil. With oil-powered tractors and harvesters, a farmer can work the land with a minimum of manual labor. And using an oil-powered aircraft, a single person can spray a large field with pesticide or herbicide in minutes. Even pesticides and herbicides, which increase crop yields, may be made from chemicals derived from oil.

OIL ON THE MOVE

To sustain our oil-reliant way of life, huge quantities of oil have to be transported around the world every day— many millions of barrels of it. Some is carried across the sea in supertankers, and some is pumped through long pipelines. But most gas stations are supplied by road tankers like this. Without such tankers to keep vehicles continually supplied with gas, countries would grind to a standstill in just a few days. A century ago the farthest most people went for a vacation was a short train ride away. Now millions of people fly huge distances, often traveling halfway around the world for a vacation of just a few weeks or less. But like cars and trucks, aircraft are fueled by oil, and the amount of oil consumed by air travel is rising all the time.

Ancient oil

In many parts of the Middle East, the region's vast underground oil reserves seep to the surface in sticky black pools and lumps. People learned long ago just how useful this black substance, called bitumen (or pitch or tar), could be. Stone Age hunters used it to attach flint arrowheads to their arrows. At least 6,500 years ago, people living in the marshes of what is now Iraq learned to add bitumen to bricks and cement to waterproof their houses against floods. Soon people realized that bitumen could be used for anything from sealing water tanks to gluing broken pots. By Babylonian times, there was a massive trade in this "black gold" throughout the Middle East, and whole cities were literally built with it.

Bamboo

Medieval painting of
Greek fishing boat

*Planks sealed
together with
bitumen*

THE FIRST OIL DRILLS
Not all ancient oil was found on the surface. Over 2,000 years ago in Sichuan, the Chinese began to drill wells. Using bamboo tipped by iron, they were able to get at brine (salty water) underground. They needed the brine to extract salt for health and preserving food. When they drilled very deep, they found not just brine but also oil and natural gas. It is not known whether the Chinese made use of the oil, but the natural gas was burned under big pans of brine to boil off the water and obtain the salt.

Chinese bamboo spring pole drilling rig

LEAK STOPPERS
About 6,000 years ago, the Ubaid people of the marshy lands in what is now Iraq realized that the qualities of bitumen made it ideal for use in waterproofing boats. They coated their reed boats with bitumen inside and out to seal them against leaks. The idea was eventually adopted by builders of wooden boats throughout the world. Known as caulking, this method was used to waterproof boats right up until the days of modern metal and fiberglass hulls. Sailors were often called "tars," because their clothes were stained with tar (bitumen) from caulking.

BABYLON BITUMEN

Most of the great buildings in Ancient Babylon relied on bitumen. To King Nebuchadnezzar (reigned 604–562 BCE), it was the most important material in the world—a visible sign of the technological achievements of his kingdom, used for everything from baths to mortar for bricks. Nowhere was it more crucial than in the Hanging Gardens, a spectacular series of roof gardens lush with flowers and trees. Bitumen was probably used as a waterproof lining for the plant beds, and also for the pipes that carried water up to them.

BLACK MUMMIES

The Ancient Egyptians preserved their dead as mummies by soaking them in a brew of chemicals such as salt, beeswax, cedar tree resin, and bitumen. The word "mummy" may come from the Arabic word *mumya*, after the Mumya Mountain in Persia where bitumen was found. Until recently, scholars believed that bitumen was never used for mummification, and that the name came simply from the way mummies turned black when exposed to air. Now, chemical analysis has shown that bitumen was indeed used in Egyptian mummies, but only during the later "Ptolemaic" period (323–30 BCE). It was shipped to Egypt from the Dead Sea, where it could be found floating on the water.

Mummified head

Frieze showing Persian archer, 510 BCE

Bow slung over shoulder

Quiver for carrying arrows

Oily cloth wrapped around arrowhead

FLAMING ARROWS

At first, people were only interested in the thick, sticky form of bitumen that was good for gluing and waterproofing. This was known as *iddu*, after the city of Hit or Id (in modern Iraq) where bitumen was found. A thinner form called *naft* (giving us the modern word naphthalene) burst into flames too readily to be useful. By the 6th century BCE, the Persians had realized that *naft* could be lethal in battle. Persian archers put it on their arrows to fire flaming missiles at their enemies. Much later, in the 6th century CE, the Byzantine navy developed this idea further. They used deadly fire bombs, called "Greek fire," made from bitumen mixed with sulfur and quicklime.

The siege of Carthage

CARTHAGE BURNING

Bitumen is highly flammable, but it is such a strong adhesive and so good at repelling water that it was used extensively on roofs in ancient cities such as Carthage. Sited on the coast of North Africa, in what is now Tunisia, Carthage was so powerful in its heyday that it rivaled Rome. Under the great leader Hannibal, the Carthaginians invaded Italy. Rome recovered and attacked Carthage in 146 BCE. When the Romans set Carthage on fire the bitumen on the roofs helped to ensure that the flames spread rapidly and completely destroyed the city.

WARM WELCOME

In the Middle Ages, when enemies tried to scale the walls of a castle or fortified town, one famous way for defenders to fend off the attackers was to pour boiling oil down on them. The first known use of boiling oil was by Jews defending the city of Jotapata against the Romans in 67 CE. Later the idea was adopted to defend castles against attack in the Middle Ages. However, the technique was probably not used very often, since oil was extremely expensive.

Silver coin from Carthage

Oil for light

FOR MILLIONS OF YEARS, the only light in the long darkness of night (aside from the stars and Moon) came from flickering fires or burning sticks. Then about 70,000 years ago, prehistoric people discovered that oils burn with a bright, steady flame. They made the first oil lamps by hollowing out a stone, filling it with moss or plant fibers soaked in oil, and then setting the moss on fire. Later, they found the lamp would burn longer and brighter if they lit just a fiber "wick" dipped in a dish of oil. The oil could be animal fat, beeswax, or vegetable oil from olives or sesame seeds. Sometimes it was actually petroleum, which prehistoric people found in small pools on the ground. Oil lamps remained the main source of lighting until the invention of the gas lamp in Victorian times.

KEROSENE LAMP

For 70 years after Aimé Argand invented his lamp (see below), most oil lamps burned whale oil. This began to change with the production of a cheaper fuel called kerosene or paraffin, from petroleum around the mid-19th century. By the early 1860s, the majority of oil lamps burned kerosene. Although fairly similar to Argand's design, a kerosene lamp has the fuel reservoir at the bottom, beneath the wick, instead of being in a separate cylinder. The size of the flame is controlled by adjusting how much of the wick extends out of the fuel reservoir.

LADIES OF THE LAMP

By the 1890s, selling kerosene for lamps was a big business, so kerosene makers tried to give their product a glamorous image. The French company Saxoleine commissioned a now-famous series of posters from the artist Jules Chéret (1836–1932). These showed various attractive Parisian women going into raptures over oil lamps filled with Saxoleine fuel, which the company claimed was clean, odorless, and safe.

Glass chimney

Glass shade to distribute the light evenly

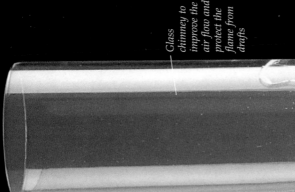

Glass chimney to improve the air flow and protect the flame from drafts

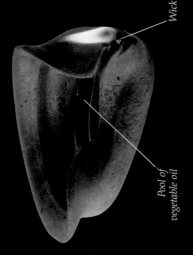

Wick

Pool of vegetable oil

LIGHT IN EGYPT

A lamp could be made by simply laying a wick over the edge of a stone bowl. When the bowl had to be handcarved from stone, lamps were probably rare. Later, people learned to mass produce bowls from pottery. They soon developed the design by pinching and pulling the edges to make a narrow neck in which the wick could lay. This is a 2,000-year-old clay lamp from Ancient Egypt.

whale oil

Wick holder

Oil inlet tube

Cup to catch oil drips

Wick height adjuster

Reservoir for paraffin

Handle

ROMAN NIGHTS
The Greeks improved lamps by putting a lid on the bowl, with just a small hole for the oil and a spout for the wick. The lid made it harder to spill the oil, and restricted the flow of air, making the oil last much longer. By the time of the Romans, every household had its array of clay and bronze lamps, often elaborately decorated. The lid of this Roman lamp shows a scene of the burning of the city of Carthage and its queen Dido.

Lid to control burning and cut spillage

Spout

ARGAND LAMP
In the 1780s, the Swiss physicist Aimé Argand (1750–1803) made the greatest breakthrough in lighting since the time of the Greeks. He realized that by placing a circular wick in the middle of an oil lamp and covering it with a chimney to improve the air flow, the lamp would burn ten times brighter than a candle and very cleanly. Argand's lamp quickly superseded all other oil lamps. It revolutionized home life, making rooms bright at night for the first time in history.

WHALE HUNT
Whales had been hunted for their meat for 2,000 years, but in the 18th century people in Europe and North America realized that the plentiful fat of whales, especially sperm whales, also gave a light oil that would burn brightly and cleanly. Demand for whale oil for use in lamps suddenly rocketed. The New England coast of northeastern America became the center of a massive whaling industry, which was made famous in Herman Melville's 1851 book *Moby Dick*.

FLAMING TORCHES
In Hollywood films, medieval castles are illuminated at night by flaming torches mounted in wall brackets called sconces. The torches were bundles of sticks dipped in resin or pitch to make them burn brighter.
In fact, torches were probably used only for special banquets, like this illustration of the Torch Dance in the *Golf Book* by Simon Bening of Bruges, c. 1500 (the torch bearers are on the far left).
For everyday light, people used lamps like those of the Ancient Egyptians, or simple rush lights—burning tapers made from rushes dipped in animal fat.

Dawn of the oil age

FOR A THOUSAND YEARS, people in the Middle East had been distilling oil to make kerosene for lamps, using small flasks called alembics. However, the modern oil age began in 1853, when a Polish chemist named Ignacy Lukasiewicz (1822–82) discovered how to do this on an industrial scale. In 1856, he set up the world's first crude oil refinery at Ulaszowice in Poland. Canadian Abraham Gesner (1791–1864) had managed to make kerosene from coal in 1846, but oil yielded it in larger quantities and more cheaply Kerosene quickly replaced the more expensive whale oil as the main lamp fuel in North America and Europe. The rising demand for kerosene produced a scramble to find new sources of oil—especially in the US.

Seneca Oil Company stock certificate

"THE YANKEE HAS STRUCK OIL!"
New York lawyer George Bissell (1812–84) was sure that liqu: oil below ground could be tapped by drilling. He formed Seneca Oil and hired Edwin L. Drake (1818–80), a retired railroad conductor, to go to Titusville, Pennsylvania, where water wells were often contaminated by oil. On August 28, 1859, Drake's men drilled down 70 ft (21 m)– and struck oil t create the US's first oil well.

THE BLACK CITY
Drilled in 1847, the world's first oil well was at Baku on the Caspian Sea, in what is now Azerbaijan. Baku soon boomed with the new demand for oil. Wells were sunk by the hundred to tap into the vast underground reserves of liquid oil nearby. Known as the Black City, Baku was producing 90 percent of the world's oil by the 1860s. This painting by Herbert Ruland shows Baku in 1960. Baku is still a major oil center.

Oil Springs, Ontario, 1862

Edwin L. Drake

Powered by an electric motor, a pair of cranks raise and lower one end of the walking beam

Pump Jack

OIL BY THE BUCKET
In 1858, James Williams (1818–90) realized that the oily black swamps of Lambton County in Ontario, Canada, might be a source of petroleum for Kerosene. He dug a hole and found that oil bubbled up so readily that he could fill bucket after bucket. This was the first oil well in the Americas. The area became known as Oil Springs, and within a few years it was dotted with simple "derricks"—frames for supporting the drilling equipment.

The curved end of the beam is likened to a harse's head in the U.S.

Nodding donkeys are still a common sight in oil fields

Driving beam operates the plunger in the well shaft as it rises and falls

Signal Hill oil field, California, 1935

THE OIL FOREST
Initially, the hunt for oil was a free-for-all, with many thousands of individuals risking all to try and strike it rich. As each prospector claimed a share of the spoils, the oil fields (areas of subterranean oil reserves) soon became covered by forests of oil wells and their tower-like derricks.

NODDING DONKEY
In the early days, the main sources of oil were only just below the surface. Countless wells were dug to get at it. Sometimes, the oil came up under its own natural pressure at first. But once enough oil was removed, the pressure dropped and the oil had to be pumped up. The typical pump was nicknamed a "nodding donkey" because of the way its driving-beam swung slowly up and down. As the "head" end of the beam falls, the pump's plunger goes down into the well. When the head rises, the plunger draws oil to the surface.

FIRE DRILL
The pioneering oil business was full of danger, and claimed the lives of many oil workers. Perhaps the greatest threat was fire. Refineries blew up, oil tanks burned down, and well heads burst into flames. Once a gusher caught fire, it was very hard to put out, because the fire was constantly fed with oil from below. This burning gusher at Jennings, Louisiana, was photographed in 1902.

SPINDLETOP DRILLERS
Most early oil wells were shallow, and the oil could only be pumped up in small quantities. Then in 1901, oil workers at Spindletop in Texas, were drilling more than 1,000 (300 m) down when they were overwhelmed by a fountain of mud and oil that erupted from the drill hole. This was Texas's first "gusher," where oil is forced up from underground by its own natural pressure. When naturally pressurized like this, oil can gush forth in enormous quantities. Modern blow-out systems now prevent uncontrolled release of oil.

Petroleum Center, Pennsylvania, 1873

BOOM TOWNS
As more and more oil wells were sunk, so whole new towns grew up to house the ever-growing armies of oil workers. Oil towns were rough, ramshackle places thrown up almost overnight. They reeked of gas fumes and were black with oil waste. Some were quite literally "boom towns," since the reckless storage of nitroglycerine used to blast open wells meant that explosions were frequent.

The oil bonanza

Bordino steam car, 1854

NOTHING TRANSFORMED THE OIL INDUSTRY more than the arrival of the motor car in the US. In 1900, there were just 8,000 cars on US roads. Car ownership reached 125,000 in 1908, and soared to 8.1 million by 1920. In 1930, there were 26.7 million cars in the US—all of which needed fuel, and that fuel was gas made from oil. Soon speculative prospectors known as "wildcatters" were drilling anywhere in the US where there was a hint that oil might be lurking. Many went broke, but the lucky ones made their fortunes by striking "gushers." Oil from California, Oklahoma, and especially Texas fueled a tremendous economic growth that soon made the US the world's richest country. As car manufacturers and oil companies prospered, the oil bonanza transformed the country forever.

STEAMED OUT

Some early cars had steam engines, not internal combustion engines like most cars today. This one, built by Virginio Bordino (1804–79) in 1854, burned coal to boil water into steam. Later steam cars burned gas or kerosene, and were far more effective, but it still took about 30 minutes to get up steam before they could move. With internal combustion engine cars, a driver could just "get in and go"—especially after the invention of the electric starter motor in 1903.

FILL HER UP!

As more and more Americans took to the wheel in the 1920s, so roadside filling stations sprang up the length and breadth of the country to satisfy the cars' insatiable thirst for fuel. In those days, cars had smaller tanks, and could not travel so far between fill-ups. Consequently, virtually every village, neighborhood, and small town, had a filling station, each with its own distinctive pumps designed in the oil company's style. These 1920s filling stations are now a cherished piece of motoring heritage.

T-TIME

Henry Ford (1863–1947) dreamed of making "a motor car for the great multitude—a car so low in price that no man making a good salary will be unable to own one." The result was Ford's Model T, the world's first mass-produced car. Launched in 1908, the T was an instant success. Within five years, there were a quarter of a million Model Ts, amounting to 50 percent of all the cars in the US. In 1925, still half of all American cars were Model Ts, but by now there were 15 million of them. The Model T created the first big boom in oil consumption.

The wings could be simply bolted in seconds as the car passed along the production

The wheels were fitted early in the production process, so that the chassis could be moved easily along the line

Every pump had an illuminated top to make it easy to see at night

The key to the T's construction was its sturdy chassis of vanadium steel

BE 2789

MASS-PRODUCTION

Cars were toys of the rich in the early 1900s. Each car was hand-built by craftsmen, and hugely expensive. All of that changed with the invention of mass-production. In mass-production, cars were not built individually. Instead, vast teams of workers added components as partly assembled cars were pulled past on factory production lines. Made like this, cars could be produced cheaply and in huge quantities. Mass-production turned the car into an everyday mode of transportation for ordinary Americans.

The Gilmore company was founded by a Los Angeles dairy farmer after he struck oil while drilling for water for his cows

Old pumps are now collectors' items, often changing hands for thousands of dollars

Display shows the price of the amount sold.

Lower counter records fuel flow

Hose delivers fuel from underground storage tank

THE BIG SELL

Black and sticky, oil is not obviously attractive. So oil companies went out of their way to give their oil a glamorous image in order to maximize sales. Advertisements used bright colors and stylish locations, and some of the best young artists of the day were hired to create wonderful looking posters. This one for Shell oils dates from 1926. The oil itself is nowhere to be seen.

In the absence of the real thing, some women even stained their legs to simulate the color of nylons

Faking nylons, 1940s

Ad portrays an idealized image of domestic life

Advertisement for Tupperware, 1950s

NYLONS

In the 1930s, companies looked for ways to use the oil leftover after motor oil had been extracted. In 1935, Wallace Carothers of the DuPont™ chemical company used oil to create a strong, stretchy artificial fiber called nylon. Launched in 1939, nylon stockings were an instant hit with young women. During the hardships of World War II (1939-45), when nylons were in short supply, women often faked nylons by drawing black "seams" down the backs of their legs.

Nylon stockings

EARLY PLASTICS

Many plastics familiar today had their origins in the oil boom, as scientists discovered they could make plastics such as PVC and polyethylene from oil. When prosperity returned after World War II, a vast range of cheap, everyday plastic products was introduced for use in the home. The most famous was "Tupperware" food storage boxes, launched by DuPont™ chemist Earl Tupper in 1946.

ROARING OIL

As oil companies vied for the new business, each company tried to create its own unique brand image. Often, the image had nothing to do with oil. Instead, it was an idea that made the oil seem more attractive or exciting. This 1930s pump from the Gilmore company, associating its gas with a lion's roar, was typical. Today, such brand imaging is common, but in the 1920s it was new.

Asphalt

STICKY STUFF
In some places, underground oil seeps up to the surface. Exposed to the air, its most volatile components evaporate to leave a black ooze or even a lump like this. When it is like thick molasses it is called bitumen; when it is like caramel it is asphalt. These forms of oil are often referred to as pitch or tar.

NATURAL GAS
Oil contains some compounds that are so volatile that they evaporate easily and form natural gas. Nearly every oil deposit contains enough of these compounds to create at least some natural gas. Some deposits contain such a high proportion that they are virtually all gas.

Natural gas flame

What is oil?

OIL AND NATURAL GAS together make up petroleum, which is Latin for "rock oil." Petroleum is a dark, oily substance that is typically liquid, but it can also be solid or gaseous. When it comes straight out of the ground as a liquid it is called crude oil if it is dark and sticky, and condensate if clear and volatile (evaporates easily). When solid it is called asphalt, and when semisolid it is called bitumen. Natural gas can be found either with oil or on its own. Petroleum is made entirely naturally, largely from the decomposed remains of living things. Although it looks like a simple gooey mass, it is actually a complex mixture of chemicals. Different chemical groups can be separated out at refineries and petrochemical plants, and then used to make a huge range of different substances.

CRUDE OIL
Crude oil is usually thick and oily, but it can come in a huge range of compositions and colors, including black, green, red, or brown. Crude oil from Sudan is jet black and North Sea oil is dark brown. Oil from the US state of Utah is amber, while oil from parts of Texas is almost straw-colored. "Sweet" crudes are oils that are easy to refine because they contain little sulfur. "Sour" oils contain more sulfur, and consequently need more processing. The color depends, for the most part, on the density (specific granity) of the oil.

Brown crude oil

Black crude oil

OIL MIXTURE
Oil mainly contains the elements hydrogen (14 percent by weight) and carbon (84 percent). These are combined in oil as chemical compounds called hydrocarbons. There are three main types of oil hydrocarbon, called alkanes, aromatics, and naphthenes. This diagram shows the approximate proportions of these substances in "Saudi heavy" crude oil, which is higher in alkanes than many crude oils.

Aromatics 15%

Alkanes 60%

Naphthenes 25%

Saudi heavy crude

Light oils float on water

Oil and water do not mix

Hydrogen atom

Carbon atom

LIGHT AND HEAVY OIL
Thin and volatile oils (crudes that readily evaporate) are described as "light," whereas thick and viscous oils (crudes that do not flow well) are said to be "heavy." Most oils float easily on water, but some heavy oils will actually sink (although not in seawater, which has a higher density than freshwater).

HYDROCARBON CHEMICALS
The hydrocarbons in crude oil have either ring- or chain-shaped molecules. Alkanes, including methane and octane, have chainlike molecules. Aromatics, such as benzene, have ring molecules, while naphthenes are heavy-ring hydrocarbons. Oil also contains tiny amounts of non-hydrogen compounds called NSOs, which are mostly nitrogen, sulfur, and oxygen.

Octane hydrocarbon molecule

COW GAS

Methane, a constituent of oil, is a naturally abundant hydrocarbon. It is a simple hydrocarbon, with each molecule consisting of just a single carbon atom attached to four hydrogen atoms. Vast quantities of methane are locked up within organic material on the seabed. The world's livestock also emit huge amounts of methane gas by flatulence. The methane forms as bacteria break down food in the animals' digestive systems.

Each group consists of one carbon atom and two hydrogen atoms

Babies could not be conceived without the hydrocarbon hormones in their parents' bodies

HYDROCARBONS IN THE BODY

There are many natural hydrocarbons in the human body. One is cholesterol, the oily, fatty substance in your blood that helps to build the walls of blood vessels. Other crucial hydrocarbons in the body include the steroid hormones, such as progesterone and testosterone, which are very important in sex and reproduction.

Rice is a good source of starch

Sugar cane is rich in sugars, which provide the body with instant energy

This chain molecule is called octane because it is made from eight carbon and hydrogen groups

SPLITTING OIL

Each of the hydrocarbons in crude oil has different properties. To make use of these properties, crude oil is refined (processed) to separate it into different groups of hydrocarbons, as seen above. The groups can be identified essentially by their density and viscosity, with bitumen being the most dense and viscous, and gas the least.

PLANT HYDROCARBONS

Hydrocarbons occur naturally in many plant oils and animal fats, too. The smells of plants and flowers are produced by hydrocarbons known as essential oils. Perfume makers often heat, steam, or crush plants to extract these essential oils for use in their scents. Essential oils called terpenes are used as natural flavoring additives in food. Moth repellents contain a terpene called camphor that moths dislike.

Lavender

Lavender's scent comes from a mix of terpene hydrocarbons

CARBOHYDRATES

People often confuse hydrocarbons and carbohydrates. Hydrocarbon molecules have a structure based on carbon and hydrogen atoms, but carbohydrates have oxygen built into their structure as well. The addition of oxygen enables them to take a huge variety of complex forms that are essential to living things. Carbohydrates such as starches and sugars are the basic energy foods of both plants and animals. Starches release energy more slowly than sugars.

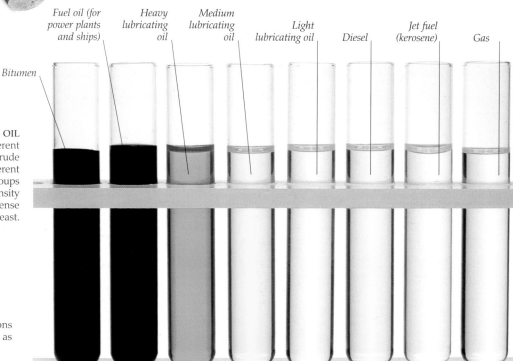

Bitumen

Fuel oil (for power plants and ships)

Heavy lubricating oil

Medium lubricating oil

Light lubricating oil

Diesel

Jet fuel (kerosene)

Gas

Where oil comes from

Scientists once thought that most oil was formed by chemical reactions between minerals in rocks deep underground. Now, the majority of scientists believe that only a little oil was formed like this. Much of the world's oil formed, they think, from the remains of living things over a vast expanse of time. The theory is that the corpses of countless microscopic marine organisms, such as foraminifera and particularly plankton, piled up on the seabed as a thick sludge, and were gradually buried deeper by sediments accumulating on top of them. There the remains were transformed over millions of years—first by bacteria and then by heat and pressure inside Earth—into liquid oil. The oil slowly seeped through the rocks and collected in underground pockets called traps, where it is tapped by oil wells today.

Magnified view of diatoms

Diatoms have glassy shells made of silica

Diatom shells come in many different shapes, and they are often complex, beautiful structures

Light greeny-blue patches are phytoplankton blooms

BLOOMING OCEAN

The formation of oil probably relies on the huge growth of plankton that often occur in the shallow ocean water off continents. Called blooms, they create thick masses of plantlike phytoplankton. The blooms can be so large that they are visible in satellite images like the one above which shows the Bay of Biscay, France. Blooms typically erupt in spring, when sunshine and an upwelling of cold, nutrient-rich water from the depth provokes explosive plankton growth.

PLANKTON SOUP

The surface waters of oceans and lakes are rich in floating plankton. Although far too small to see with the naked eye, plankton are so abundant that their corpses form thick blankets on the seabed. There are two main types of plankton. Phytoplankton, like plants, can make their own food using sunlight. Zooplankton feed on phytoplankton and on each other. The most abundant phytoplankton are called diatoms.

CONCENTRATED POWER SOURCE

Oil is packed with energy, stored in the bonds that hold its hydrocarbon molecules together. Ultimately, all this energy comes from the sun. Long ago, tiny organisms called phytoplankton used energy from sunlight to convert simple chemicals into food in a process called photosynthesis. As the dead phytoplankton were changed into oil, this trapped energy became ever more concentrated.

18

Chalk cliffs containing fossilized foraminifera, Sussex, England

TEST CASE
Tiny one-celled organisms called foraminifera, or "forams," are abundant throughout the world's oceans. Like diatoms, they are a prime source material for oil. Forams secrete a shell or casing around themselves called a test. Chalk rock is rich in fossilized foram shells. Every era and rock layer seemed to have its own special foram, so oil prospectors look for forams when drilling to gain an insight into the history of the rock.

Microscopic foram shell with pores

Shell is made of calcium carbonate

Microscopic view of kerogen particle

HOW OIL FORMS
The buried marine organisms are first rotted by bacteria into substances called kerogen and bitumen. As kerogen and bitumen are buried deeper—between 3,300 and 10,000 ft (1,000 and 6,000 m)—heat and pressure "cook" them. This turns them into bubbles of oil and natural gas. The bubbles are spread throughout porous rock, like water in a sponge. Over millions of years, some of them seep up through the rock, collecting in traps when they meet impermeable rock layers.

Marine organisms die and are buried underneath the seafloor

Oil and natural gas form in porous sedimentary rock

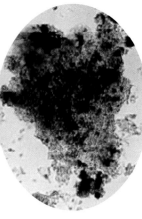

HALFWAY STAGE
Just a small proportion of the buried remains of microscopic marine organisms turns into oil. Most only undergoes the first stage of transformation, into kerogen. This is a browny-black solid found in sedimentary rocks (those formed from the debris of other rocks and living things). To turn into oil, kerogen must be heated under pressure to more than 140°F (60°C).

OIL IN SPACE
Could oil-like rings and chains of hydrocarbons form in space? After analyzing the color of light from distant stars, astronomers believe that they very well might. Observations by the Infrared Space Observatory satellite of the dying star CRL618 in 2001 detected the presence of benzene, which has the classic ring-shaped hydrocarbon molecule.

Oil and gas migrate upward

Impermeable rock does not let oil or gas pass through

Trapped gas

Trapped oil

Natural gas

THOUSANDS OF YEARS AGO, people in parts of Greece, Persia, and India noticed a gas seeping from the ground that caught fire very easily. These natural gas flames sometimes became the focus of myths or religious beliefs. Natural gas is a mixture of gases, but it contains mostly methane—the smallest and lightest hydrocarbon. Like oil, natural gas formed underground from the remains of tiny marine organisms, and it is often brought up at the same wells as crude oil. It can also come from wells that contain only gas and condensate, or from "natural" wells that provide natural gas alone. Little use was made of natural gas until fairly recently. In the early 20th century, oil wells burned it off as waste. Today, natural gas is highly valued as a clean fuel that supplies a quarter of the world's energy.

WILL-O'-THE-WISP

When organic matter rots, it may release a gas (now called biogas) that is a mixture of methane and phosphine. Bubbles of biogas seeping from marshes and briefly catching fire gave birth to the legend of the "will-o'-the-wisp"—ghostly lights said be used by spirits or demons to lure travelers to their doom, as seen here.

EXTRACTION AND PROCESSING

Natural gas is often extracted at plants like the one below. The gas is so light that it rises up the gas well without any need for pumping. Before being piped away for use, it has to be processed to remove impurities and unwanted elements. "Sour gas," which is high in sulfur and carbon dioxide, is highly corrosive and dangerous, so it needs extra processing. Because processed natural gas has no smell, substances called thiols are added to give it a distinct odor so that leaks can be detected.

Worker inspecting a natural gas pipe, Russia

PIPING GAS

Most natural gas brought up from underground is transported by pipeline. Major gas pipelines are assembled from sections of carbon steel, each rigorously tested for pressure resistance. Gas is pumped through the pipes under immense pressure. The pressure not only reduces the volume of the gas to be transported by up to 600 times, but it also provides the "push" to move the gas through the pipe.

A typical LNG tanker holds more than 40 million gallons (150 million liters) of LNG, with an energy content equivalent to 24 billion gallons (91 billion liters) of the gaseous form

Extraction and processing plant at gas field near Noviy Urengoy, western Siberia, Russia

Processing units clean the gas of impurities and unwanted substances

STREET REVOLUTION

The introduction of gas street lamps to London, England, in the early years of the 19th century marked the beginning of a revolution. Before long, city streets the world over— once almost totally dark at night—were filled with bright, instant light. Although natural gas was used for street lighting as early as 1816, most 19th-century street lamps burned a gas known as coal gas, which was made from coal. Electricity began to replace gas for street lighting during the early 20th century.

GAS TANKER

Not all gas travels through pipelines—especially when it has to go to far-off destinations overseas. Huge ships equipped with spherical storage tanks carry gas across the ocean in a form called liquid natural gas, or LNG. This is made by cooling natural gas to –260°F (160°C). At that temperature, natural gas becomes liquid. As a liquid, its volume is less than 1/600th of its volume as a gas.

Gas lamps had to be lit individually each night

TOWN GAS

By the mid-18th century, most towns had their own gas works for making coal gas, or "town gas" as it was also known. The gas was stored in vast metal tanks called gasometers, which became familiar sights in urban areas. In addition to lighting, town gas had many other uses, including cooking and heating. Town gas fell out of use in the second half of the 20th century, after the discovery of vast natural gas fields and the building of pipelines had made natural gas more widely available. Natural gas was also cheaper and safer to use than town gas.

Gasometers sank into the ground as the level of gas inside went down

Heavily reinforced tanks keep the gas pressurized and in liquid form

Propane burns with a blue flame

GAS CAVE

Natural gas is too bulky and flammable to store in tanks. After being processed and piped to its destination, the gas is stored underground ready for use, sometimes in old salt mines like this one in Italy. Other subterranean storage sites include aquifers (rock formations that hold water) and depleted gas reservoirs (porous rock that once held "raw" natural gas).

A single tank contains enough energy to meet all the US's electricity needs for five minutes

Processed natural gas is pumped into pipes for distribution

GAS SPIN OFFS

Gases such as ethane, propane, butane, and isobutane are removed from natural gas during processing. Most of these gases are sold separately. Propane and butane, for example, are sold in canisters as fuel for camping stoves. A few gas wells also contain helium. Best known for its use in balloons, helium also acts as a coolant in a range of devices, from nuclear reactors to body scanners.

Unconventional natural gas

NATURAL GAS IS THE CLEANEST BURNING of the fossil fuels, and natural gas has become a preferred fuel for electricity generation. Demand is rising so quickly that producers are struggling to keep up. In the future, more and more natural gas will come from unconventional sources. Unconventional natural gas is more difficult and less economical to extract than conventional natural gas. At the same time, unconventional wells are productive longer than conventional wells and can contribute to sustaining supply over a longer period. The gas is essentially the same substance as conventional natural gas, and has the same uses, such as electricity generation, heating, cooking, transportation, and products for industrial and domestic use. New technologies are continually being developed to provide more accurate estimations of the amount of gas in these unconventional reservoirs and to stimulate the reservoirs to produce the gas. What are unconventional today may be conventional tomorrow through advances in technology or new innovative processes.

The worms are a new species—colonies of these one-to-two inch long, pinkish worms live on and within mounds of methane ice on the floor of the Gulf of Mexico

METHANE HYDRATES

Methane hydrates are a cage-like lattice of ice formed around methane molecules. They form at low temperature and high pressure. They are found in sea-floor sediments and the arctic permafrost. They look like ice, but form above the freezing point of water. They burn when touched by a lit match. Some believe there is enough methane hydrates to supply energy for hundreds, maybe thousands of years. If only one percent of the methane hydrate resource could be technically and economically recoverable, the U.S. could more than double its domestic natural gas resource.

Bermuda

Miami

Bermuda Triangle

San Juan Puerto Rico

Caribbean Sea

Gas hydrates are found densely around the Bermuda triangle, and could have caused ships to sink, but it is a myth that many ships have sunk there.

440 trillion cubic meters — world conventional natural gas accumulations

3,000 trillion cubic meters — estimated world gas hydrate accumulations

Source: U.S. Geological Survey World Petroleum Assessment 2000.

COAL GASIFICATION

Coal gasification is a process for converting coal into combustible gases by breaking it down into its basic chemical constituents. After purification these gases—carbon monoxide, carbon dioxide, hydrogen, methane, and nitrogen—can be used as fuels or as raw materials for energy products.

Gasification may be one of the best ways to produce clean-burning hydrogen for tomorrow's automobiles. It also offers efficiency gains. Heat from burning coal can be used to boil water, making steam that drives a steam turbine generator. The first commercial coal gasification electric power plants are now operating. Many experts believe gasification will be the heart of future generations clean coal technology plants for several decades.

DEEP GAS

Deep gas is natural gas that exists in underground deposits, typically 15,000 feet or deeper. Much deep gas is located in undersea reservoirs, so the well must extend over 15,000 feet, and the drill string must also pass through hundreds or thousands of feet of seawater.

This coal-gasification power plant in Tampa, Florida, uses coal to create a clean-burning gas. The technology removes at least 95 percent of the sulfur from the coal gas.

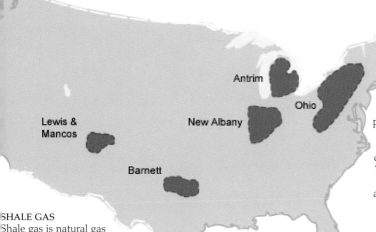

TIGHT GAS

Tight gas, also called "low perm sandstone," is gas stuck in a tight formation underground, trapped in unusually low permeability and low porosity hard rock, sandstone, or limestone. The rock layers are dense, so the gas does not flow easily through them. Techniques that extract natural gas from these formations are costly and difficult. It can be compared to drilling a hole into concrete.

Photo: Anadarko Petroleum Corporation

SHALE GAS

Shale gas is natural gas stored in rocks dominated by shale, a fine-grained sedimentary rock. It is usually found over large, contiguous areas where a thin layer of shale sets between two thick, black shale deposits. It can be stored as a free gas within the rock pores or natural fractures, or as adsorbed gas on organic material. The rocks containing shale gas have low permeability, making the gas difficult to release. The first commercial gas shale well was drilled in New York in the late 1820s. Today over 28,000 gas shale wells produce nearly 380 billion cubic feet of gas yearly from five U.S. basins: Appalachian, Michigan, Illinois, Fort Worth, and San Juan.

Photo: Canadian Society for Unconventional Gas

COALBED METHANE

Coalbed methane (CBM) is methane found in underground coal seams. The near-liquid methane lines the inside of the coal's pores and is held in by water pressure. When water is pumped to relieve pressure, the methane separates and can be piped out of the well separately from the water. CBM can be recovered economically, but disposal of water is an environmental concern. Coalbed methane is generally released during coal mining, creating dangerous conditions for coal miners.

In the past, the methane was intentionally vented into the atmosphere. Today, however, methane can be extracted and injected into natural gas pipelines. The Southern Ute American Indian tribe's 700,000-acre reservation in the San Juan Basin sits on one of the world's richest deposits of coalbed methane. They currently control the distribution of roughly one percent of the U.S. natural gas supply, and are a model for other resource-based tribes.

GEOPRESSURIZED ZONES

Geopressurized zones are underground natural gas deposits that are under unusually high pressure for their depth. They contain layers of sand or silt and are located between 15,000 and 25,000 feet below the earth's surface, either under dry land or beneath sea beds. Geopressurized zones form when layers of clay are deposited and quickly compacted on top of more porous, absorbent material such as sand or silt. Rapid compression of the clay and high pressure squeezes out any water and natural gas into the more porous deposits. No commercial extraction technique has been developed, and only exploratory drillings have been made.

Oil traps

WHEN OIL COMPANIES DRILL FOR OIL, they look for oil traps. These are places where oil collects underground after seeping up through the surrounding rocks. This slow seepage, called migration, begins soon after liquid oil first forms in a "source" rock. Shales, rich in solid organic matter known as kerogen, are the most common type of source rock. The oil forms when the kerogen is altered by heat and pressure deep underground. As source rocks become buried ever deeper over time, oil and gas may be squeezed out like water from a sponge and migrate through permeable rocks. These are rocks with tiny cracks through which fluids can seep. The oil is frequently mixed with water and, since oil floats on water, the oil tends to migrate upward. Sometimes, though, it comes up against impermeable rock, through which it cannot pass. Then it becomes trapped and slowly accumulates, forming a reservoir.

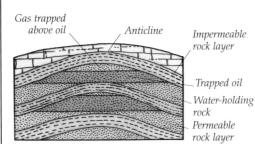

Gas trapped above oil — Anticline — Impermeable rock layer — Trapped oil — Water-holding rock — Permeable rock layer

ANTICLINE TRAP
Oil is often trapped under anticlines—places where layers (strata) of rock have been bent up into an arch by the movement of Earth's crust. If one of these bent layers is impermeable, the oil may ooze up underneath it and accumulate there. Anticline traps like this hold much of the world's oil.

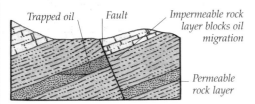

Trapped oil — Fault — Impermeable rock layer blocks oil migration — Permeable rock layer

FAULT TRAP
Every now and then, rock strata crack and slide up or down past each other. This is known as a fault. Faults can create oil traps in various ways. The most common is when the fault slides a layer of impermeable rock across a layer of permeable rock through which oil is migrating.

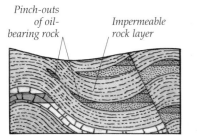

Pinch-outs of oil-bearing rock — Impermeable rock layer

PINCH-OUT TRAPS
Anticline, fault, and salt-dome traps are created by the arrangement of the rock layers, and are called structural traps. Stratigraphic traps are created by variations within the rock layers themselves. A pinch-out is a common type of stratigraphic trap. Pinch-out traps are often formed from old stream beds, where a lens-shaped region of permeable sand becomes trapped within less permeable shales and siltstones.

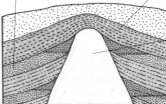

Permeable rock layer — Impermeable rock layer — Impermeable salt dome blocks path of oil — Trapped oil

SALT-DOME TRAP
When masses of salt form deep underground, heat and pressure cause them to bulge upward in domes. The rising domes force the overlying rock layers aside. As they do so, they can cut across layers of permeable rock, blocking the path of any migrating oil and creating an oil trap.

Rock strata (layers)

ROCK BENDS
It seems amazing that layers of solid rock can be bent, but the movement of the huge tectonic plates that make up Earth's crust (outer layer) generates incredible pressures. The layers of sedimentary rock exposed here in this road cutting originally formed flat from sediments deposited on the seabed. The dramatic arch, or anticline, was created as giant slabs of crust moved relentlessly together, crumpling the rock layers between. Countless anticline arches like this around the world become traps for oil.

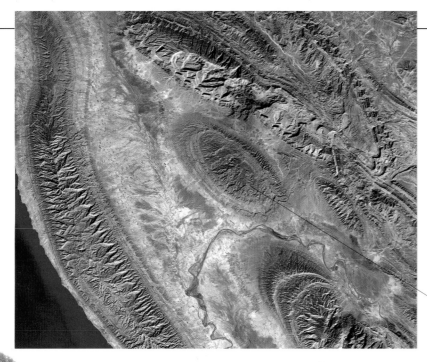

VIEW FROM ABOVE
Anticlines often form long domes that are visible as ovals on geological maps or in satellite photographs. Here a satellite photograph reveals a series of oval anticline domes in the Zagros Mountains of southwestern Iran. Each dome forms a separate, tapering mini-mountain range, looking from above like a giant half melon. Such domes would be prime targets for oil prospectors looking for major oil deposits, and the Zagros mountains are indeed one of the world's oldest and richest oil fields.

Anticline dome

TRAP ROCK
Oil will go on migrating through permeable rocks until its path is blocked by impermeable rocks—rocks in which the pores are too small or the cracks too narrow or too disconnected for oil or water to seep through. Where impermeable rock seals oil into a trap, it is called trap rock (or cap rock). The trap rock acts like the lid on the oil reservoir. The most common trap rock is shale.

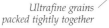

Shale

Ultrafine grains packed tightly together

Anticline (arch-shaped upfold)

Rock darkened by the organic content from which oil can form

RESERVOIR ROCKS
The oil created in source rocks only becomes accessible once it has migrated to rocks that have plenty of pores and cracks for oil to move through and accumulate in. Rocks where oil accumulates are called reservoir rocks. Most reservoir rocks, such as sandstone and to a lesser extent limestone and dolomite, have fairly large grains. The grains are loosely packed, allowing oil to seep between them.

Sandstone

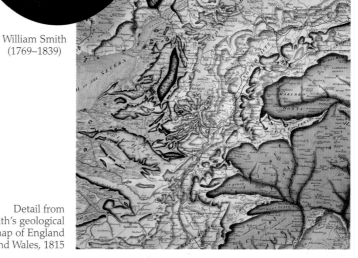

William Smith
(1769–1839)

Each rock type is shown in a particular color

Detail from Smith's geological map of England and Wales, 1815

Dolomite

Pea-sized grains

Pisolitic limestone

SMITH'S LAYERS
The knowledge of rock layers so crucial to the search for oil began with William Smith, an English canal engineer who made the first geological maps. As Smith was surveying routes for canals, he noticed that different rock layers contained particular fossils. He realized that if layers some distance apart had the same fossils, then they must be the same age. This enabled him to trace rock layers right across the landscape, and understand how they had been folded and faulted.

Solid oil

MOST OF THE OIL THE WORLD USES is black, liquid crude oil drawn up from subterranean formations. Yet this is just a tiny fraction of the oil that lies below ground. A vast quantity of more solid oil exists underground in the form of oil sands and oil shales. Oil sands (once known as tar sands) are sand and clay deposits in which each grain is covered by sticky bitumen oil. Oil shales are rocks steeped in kerogen—the organic material that turns to liquid oil when cooked under pressure. Extracting oil from oil shales and oil sands involves heating them so that the oil drains out. At the moment, it is economical, but many experts believe that when crude oil reserves begin to run out, oil shales and oil sands may become our main sources of oil.

EXTRACTION TECHNIQUES
If oil sands are near the surface, they are mined by digging a huge pit. Giant trucks carry the sand to a large machine that breaks up the lumps in the sand, then mixes it with hot water to make a slurry. The slurry is sent by pipeline to a separation plant, where the oil is removed from the sand for processing at a refinery. However, if the sands are too deep to dig out, oil companies may try to extract just the oil by injecting steam. The steam melts the bitumen and helps to separate it from the sand. It is then pumped to the surface and sent off for processing. Another method is to inject oxygen to start a fire and melt the oil. These techniques are still experimental.

Each truck carries 400 tons of sandy bitumen, the equivalent of 200 barrels of crude oil

These trucks are the biggest in the world, each weighing 400 tons

MUCKY SAND
Oil sands look like black, very sticky mud. Each grain of sand is covered by a film of water surrounded by a "slick" of bitumen. In winter, the water freezes, making the sand as hard as concrete. In summer, when the water melts, the sand becomes sticky.

ATHABASCA OIL SANDS
Oil sands are found in many places around the world, but the world's largest deposits are in Alberta, Canada, and in Venezuela, which each have about a third of the world's oil sands. Alberta, though, is the only place where the oil sands are extracted in any quantity, because the deposit at Athabasca (representing 10 percent of Alberta's oil sands) is the only one near enough to the surface to be dug out economically.

STICKY END

Tar pits, or more correctly asphalt pits, are hollows where slightly runny asphalt seeps up through the ground to create a sticky black pool. Remarkably complete fossils of prehistoric *Smilodons* (saber-toothed tigers) and their mammoth prey have been found together in tar pits, such as the famous La Brea pit in California. It seems that the mammoths got stuck in the pool and the *Smilodons*, pursuing their prey, followed them in and became stuck too.

Fossilized *Smilodon* skull

Smilodons maul a mammoth in a tar pit

Smilodon is sometimes known as the "saber-toothed tiger" because of its pair of saberlike teeth, which were used for ripping flesh

Pitch Lake, Trinidad

SCOTTISH OIL

The modern oil industry began in Scotland in 1848, when James Young (1811–83) found a way of producing kerosene for lamps using oil taken from seeps. Oil seeps were rare in Britain, so Young turned to an oil shale found in the Scottish lowlands called cannel coal, or torbanite. In 1851, he set up the world's first oil refinery at Bathgate near Edinburgh to distill oil from torbanite mined nearby.

Oil shales are turned black by kerogen held in pores in the rock

Marlstone, a type of oil shale

PITCHING IN

Trinidad's Pitch Lake is a huge natural lake of asphalt thought to be 250 ft (75 m) deep. The lake is believed to be above the intersection of two faults (cracks in the rock bed), through which the asphalt oozes up from deep underground. The English explorer Sir Walter Raleigh spotted the lake on his travels to the Caribbean in 1595, and used its asphalt to waterproof his ships for his homeward journey.

Sir Walter Raleigh (1552–1618)

OILY ROADS

The Ancient Babylonians used bitumen to make smooth, waterproof roads 2,500 ago. Modern road surfaces date from the early 19th century, when road builders began making roads with gravel bound together by hot coal tar or bitumen. The material was called tarmacadam, or tarmac, because the tar was added to a mix of graded gravel devised by John Loudon McAdam (1756–1836), a Scottish road engineer.

OIL SHALE

Although there are vast deposits of oil shale, notably in Colorado, it is hard to extract oil from them. The kerogen has to be melted out and then turned into oil by intense heat in a process called retorting. The rock can be mined and retorted on the surface, but this is expensive. Engineers think that in the future it may be possible to melt the oil out using electric heaters inserted into the rock.

How oil is found

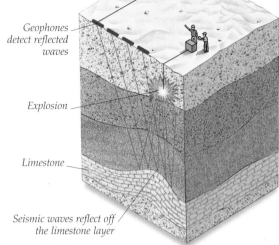

Truck with recording equipment

Geophones detect reflected waves

Explosion

Limestone

Seismic waves reflect off the limestone layer

OIL SHAKES
Seismic surveys send powerful vibrations, or seismic waves, through the ground from an explosion or a sound generator. Surveyors record how the waves reflect back to the surface off subterranean rocks. Different rock types reflect seismic waves differently, so surveyors can build up a detailed picture of the rock structure from the pattern of reflections.

In the past, finding oil except close to where it seeped visibly to the surface was largely a matter of guesswork and sheer luck. Today, oil prospectors use their knowledge of the way geology creates oil traps to guide them to areas where oil is likely to occur. They know, for example, that oil is likely to be found in one of the 600 or so basins of sedimentary rock around the world, and it is in these basins that oil exploration tends to be concentrated. So far, about 160 basins have yielded oil, and 240 have drawn a blank. Hunting for oil within sedimentary basins might begin by examining exposed rock outcrops for likely looking formations, or scanning satellite and radar images. Once a target area has been located, oil hunters carry out geophysical surveys that use sophisticated equipment to detect subtle clues such as variations in Earth's magnetic and gravitational fields created by the presence of oil.

HUNTING UNDER THE SEA
Seismic surveys can also be used to hunt for oil under the seabed. Boats tow cables attached to sound detectors called hydrophones. In the past, the vibrations were made by dynamite explosions, but this killed too many sea creatures. Now the vibrations are set off by releasing bubbles of compressed air, which send out sound waves as they expand and contract while rising to the surface.

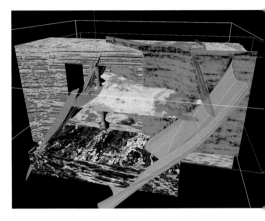

COMPUTER MODELING
The most sophisticated seismic surveys use numerous probes to survey the deep structures in a particular area. The results are then fed into a computer and used to build up a detailed 3-D model, known as a volume, of underground rock formations. Such 3-D models are expensive to generate, but drilling a well in the wrong place can waste millions of dollars.

Computer-model of rock formations

Hydraulic pads send vibrations through ground

Soft tires for travel over rough terrain

Weights to keep truck balanced

Photo: Petrobras

THUMPING TRUCKS
With seismic surveys on land, the vibrations are set off either by small explosive charges in the ground or by special trucks. These trucks, which are known as vibes, have a hydraulic pad that shakes the ground with tremendous force, at a rate of 5 to 80 times per second. The vibrations, which are clearly audible, penetrate deep into the ground. They reflect back to the surface and are picked up by detectors, called geophones.

Screws to adjust spring tension

Inside a gravimeter is a weight suspended from springs

Screen shows slight variations in the stretching of the springs caused by gravitational differences

USING GRAVITY

Rocks of different densities have a slightly different gravitational pull. Gravity meters, or gravimeters, can measure these minute differences at the surface using a weight suspended from springs. They can detect variations as small as one part in 10 million. These differences reveal features such as salt domes and masses of dense rock underground, helping geologists to build up a complete picture of the subsurface rock structure.

MAGNETIC SEARCH

Magnetic searches are usually conducted using an aircraft like this, which is equipped with a device called a magnetometer. The magnetometer detects variations in the magnetism of the ground below. The sedimentary rocks where oil is likely to be found are generally much less magnetic than rocks that form volcanically, which are rich in magnetic metals such as iron and nickel.

The drilling rig begins, or "spuds in," a new well

TEST DRILL

In the past, "wildcat" wells were drilled in places where the oil hunters had little more than a hunch that oil might be found. Today, test drilling is carried out in locations where the results of surveying suggest that there is a reasonable likelihood of an oil strike. Even so, the chances of finding quantities of oil or gas that can be commercially exploited are less than one in five.

BORE SAMPLE

Drilling is the only way to be sure that an oil or gas field exists, and exactly what kind of oil is present. Once a test drill has been bored, the oil prospectors use downhole logging equipment, which detects the physical and chemical nature of the rocks. Rock samples are brought to the surface for detailed analysis in the laboratory.

Illustration: Occidental Petroleum Corporation

Advanced technology

Eɴᴇʀɢʏ ᴄᴏᴍᴘᴀɴɪᴇs ᴀʀᴇ ᴀᴍᴏɴɢ the highest users of computing power and data of any industry except the military. Exploration specialists use data to interpret geologic structures miles beneath the earth's surface. Engineers can drill through more than five miles of rock to reach resources at extreme depths at high temperatures and pressures. Production engineers bring oil and gas to the surface through miles of production piping, also under extreme conditions, and deliver them through more miles of pipelines to refineries. Once there, increasingly "heavy" and sulfurous crude oils are refined into useful products. Advanced technologies like satellites, global positioning systems, remote sensing devices and 3-D and 4-D seismic make it possible to discover oil reserves while drilling fewer wells, resulting in a smaller environmental "footprint" and more economically than ever before. The answer to where oil is found – in computers!

HORIZONTAL DRILLING
In addition to drilling vertically, operators can now drill horizontally miles in any direction from a single starting well. By drilling several wells from a one location, the amount of land surface required to develop a field can be reduced and the well can be placed where it will have the least possible environmental impact. In Alaska, the same number of wells that required 65 acres in 1977 can be drilled in less than nine acres today. Offshore, many wells can be drilled from a single platform. In addition, horizontal drilling allows oil to be reached that is located in very thin reservoirs. It also allows more exposure of the wellbore to the producing zone, thereby increasing recoverable volumes and further limiting the need for additional wells.

DRILLING ACCURACY
Multiple wells can now be drilled from a single platform with astonishing accuracy. An engineer sitting in a control room in Houston can electronically steer a drillbit from a platform of the coast of Africa into a space the size of an average bedroom. Technological advances have greatly improved drilling success and have meant fewer wells must be drilled to produce an equal, or greater, volume of oil. The cost-savings are enormous, since a single misplaced well can cost upwards of $100 million or more offshore.

GETTING MORE OUT
Ironically, most of the oil to be discovered has already been found. Typically, oil companies can only produce one barrel for every three that they find. Two are left behind because they are too hard to pump out or because it would cost too much to do so. Going after these remaining resources represents a tremendous opportunity. Now, 4-D seismic has added the dimension of time, taking snapshots of a reservoir over time so changes in a reservoir during production can be viewed. New technology like 4-D seismic will help get even more out of the ground, boosting oil reserves and production.

Photo: Shell Photographic Services, Shell International Ltd.

In a digital oilfield, the subsea layout includes a digital control/monitoring system that transmits data from the well via satellite to a remote decision center where an asset team can make real-time decisions to improve well performance.

DIGITAL OILFIELD

A revolutionary development is real-time monitoring of what's going on in the well during both drilling and production. Smart drilling systems have sensors and measurement devices on the drill string near the drill bit that allow drillers to measure down-hole conditions in real-time. Data is streamed back to the drilling platform and then beamed back to team at the home office in Houston or Aberdeen, allowing them to make changes to drilling program moment-by-moment. These sensing devices must be very tough to withstand the shocks and extreme conditions of drilling. Likewise, smart producing wells are similarly monitored, modeled, controlled and reconfigured from remote locations.

DRILLING ON MARS

Many of the techonological developments in the oil and gas industry have found applications in other high-tech fields, including the space program. NASA is using petroleum drilling technology in its program to explore Mars. NASA is currently running five separate projects using drilling machines designed to be used in unmanned planetary space expeditions. The drilling machines are controlled by artificial intelligence and designed to drill into ice layers and permafrost that are similar to the imagined sub-surface in Martian polar regions.

Photo: NASA Ames Research Center

NANOTECHNOLOGY

Nanotechnology creates and manipulates matter at the molecular level that Nanotechnology creates and manipulates matter at the molecular level that makes it possible to create materials with improved properties, such as being both lightweight and having ultrahigh strength, and greater capabilities such as in electrical and heat conductivity. Many applications are possible for the energy industry. An advanced fluid mixed with nanosized particles and superfine powder is being researched that significantly improves drilling speed. Silicon carbide, a ceramic powder, could be made in nano size, yielding exceptionally hard materials that can contribute to harder, more wear-resistant and more durable drilling equipment. In the future, the industry may use nanoscale sensors for probing properties deep in the reservoir. The oil industry already uses nanoscale catalysts for refining petroleum, and nanoparticles with unique catalytic capabilities are being researched to more effectively and efficiently refine thick, gooey oil sands into highly refined oil.

SEEING IN 3-D

A team of geologists and geophysicists, together with reservoir, production and drilling engineers, as well as business partners, can be immersed in a common 3-D visual environment. With a click of the mouse they can explore massive geologic formations, grab a block of rock and zoom into it to see what it may hold. The journey is played out on a giant curved computer screen powered by a bank of high-end computers and graphics software that would make a video gamer jealous. Wireless and satellite data expand the ability for global collaboration, allowing a team in the office and team on a platform to share data and act on complex technical information together.

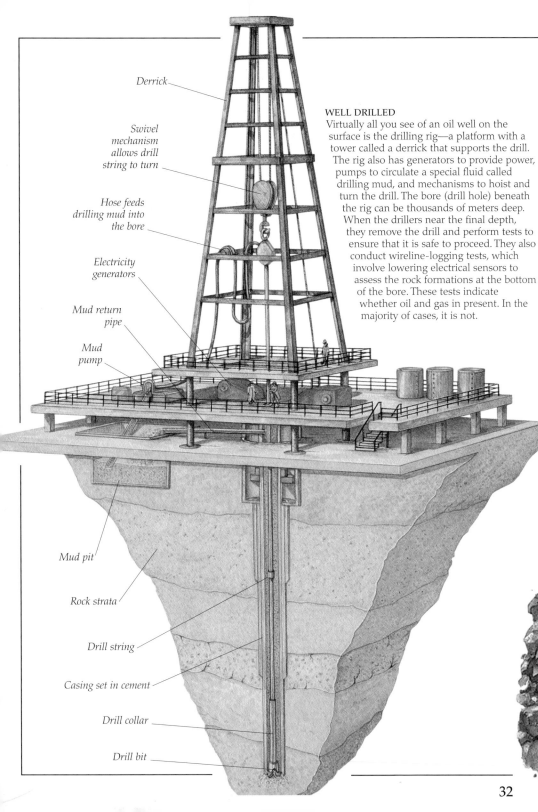

Derrick

Swivel mechanism allows drill string to turn

Hose feeds drilling mud into the bore

Electricity generators

Mud return pipe

Mud pump

Mud pit

Rock strata

Drill string

Casing set in cement

Drill collar

Drill bit

WELL DRILLED
Virtually all you see of an oil well on the surface is the drilling rig—a platform with a tower called a derrick that supports the drill. The rig also has generators to provide power, pumps to circulate a special fluid called drilling mud, and mechanisms to hoist and turn the drill. The bore (drill hole) beneath the rig can be thousands of meters deep. When the drillers near the final depth, they remove the drill and perform tests to ensure that it is safe to proceed. They also conduct wireline-logging tests, which involve lowering electrical sensors to assess the rock formations at the bottom of the bore. These tests indicate whether oil and gas in present. In the majority of cases, it is not.

Getting the oil out

LOCATING A SUITABLE SITE for drilling is just the first step in extracting oil. Before drilling can begin, companies must make sure that they have the legal right to drill, and that the impact of drilling on the environment is acceptable. This can take years. Once they finally have the go ahead, drilling begins. The exact procedure varies, but the idea is first to drill down to just above where the oil is located. Then they insert a casing of concrete into the newly drilled hole to make it stronger. Next, they make little holes in the casing near the bottom, which will let oil in, and top the well with a special assembly of control—and safety-valves called a "Christmas tree." Finally, they may send down acid or pressurized sand to break through the last layer of rock and start the oil flowing into the well.

Mud is pumped down inside the drill string

The mud travels back up the bore, taking rock cuttings with it

DIAMOND TEETH
Right at the bottom end of the string is the drill bit, which turns continuously and cuts slowly into the rock. Different rocks call for different designs of drill bit. The cutting edges of the teeth are toughened with different combinations of steel, tungsten-carbide, diamond, or PDC (synthetic diamond), according to the type of rock to be drilled.

Nozzle sprays mud on to the drill bit

RED ADAIR
Paul Neal "Red" Adair (1915–2004) was world-renowned for his exploits in fighting oil-well fires. The Texan's most famous feat was tackling a fire in the Sahara Desert in 1962, an exploit retold in the John Wayne movie *Hellfighters* (1968). When oil wells in Kuwait caught fire during the Gulf War of 1991, it was the veteran Red Adair, then aged 77, who was called in to put them out.

Fire is fed by pressurized oil and gas

STRING AND MUD
Drilling thousands of meters into solid rock is a tricky business. Unlike a hand-drill, an oil drilling rig does not have a single drilling rod, but a long "string" made from hundreds of pieces, added on one by one as the drill goes deeper. Drilling mud is pumped continuously around the drill to minimize friction. The mud also cools and cleans the drill bit, and carries the "cuttings" (drilled rock fragments) back up to the surface.

FIRE FOUNTAIN
The force of a blowout can be so great that it wrecks the drilling rig. Improved drilling techniques have made blowouts rare. If the blowout ignites, it burns fiercely, and the fire is difficult to extinguish. Fortunately, there are now only a handful of blowout fires around the world each year.

Screen protects firefighters as they tackle the blaze

Deep sea drilling

SOMETIMES LARGE RESERVES OF OIL are found deep beneath the ocean bed. To get the oil out, huge platforms are built far out at sea to provide a base for drilling rigs that bore right down into the rocks of the seafloor. After processing on the platform oil is sent ashore via pipelines or held in separate floating storage facilities before being off-loaded into large tankers. Offshore oil rigs are gigantic structures. Many have legs that stretch hundreds of meters from the surface to the ocean floor. The Petronius Platform in the Gulf of Mexico, for example, is the world's tallest free-standing structure, standing some 2,000 ft (610 m) above the seabed. Rigs have to be immensely strong, able to withstand gale-force winds and relentless pounding by huge waves.

Photo: Petro-Canada

ICEBERG TOWING
Significant reserves have been found in "iceberg alley" off the coast of Newfoundland, where winter storms with winds of nearly 100 mph can produce waves of 90 ft (30 m), and there is the ever present fog that can reduce visibility to zero. Oil platforms either can't move or require a great deal of time to move so the impact of icebergs on their operations is enormous. If an iceberg is forecast to affect oil operations, a powerful tug is dispatched to hook up a tow rope and apply force in the direction you wish to steer the iceberg. That small change will ensure the iceberg to passes safely by the platform.

RIGOROUS MAINTENANCE
Any fault in the structure of an oil rig—such as parts that have come loose or been weakened by rust—could spell disaster. The rig's engineers must maintain their vigilance around the clock, checking the structure over and over again for any signs of problems. Here they are being lowered from the platform to inspect the rig's legs for cracks after a heavy storm.

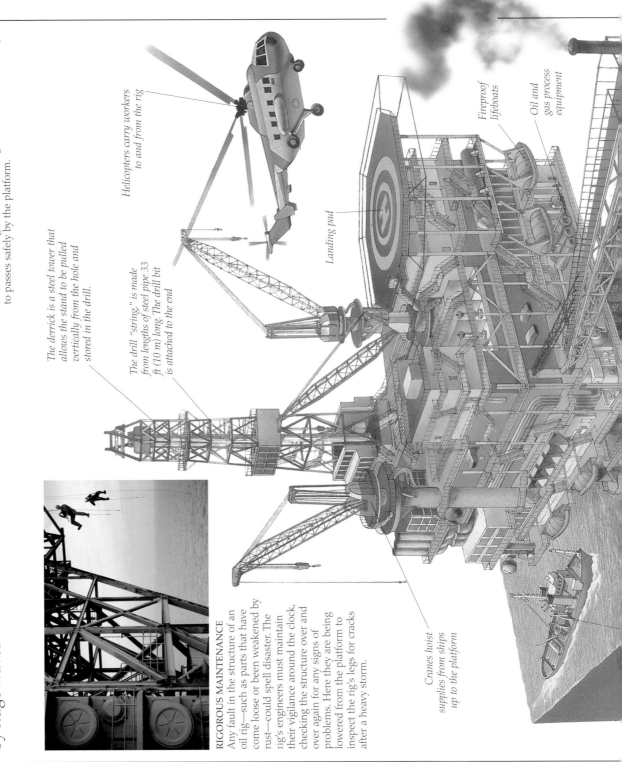

Helicopters carry workers to and from the rig

Landing pad

Fireproof lifeboats

Oil and gas process equipment

The derrick is a steel tower that allows the stand to be pulled vertically from the hole and stored in the drill.

The drill "string," is made from lengths of steel pipe 33 ft (10 m) long. The drill bit is attached to the end

Cranes hoist supplies from ships up to the platform

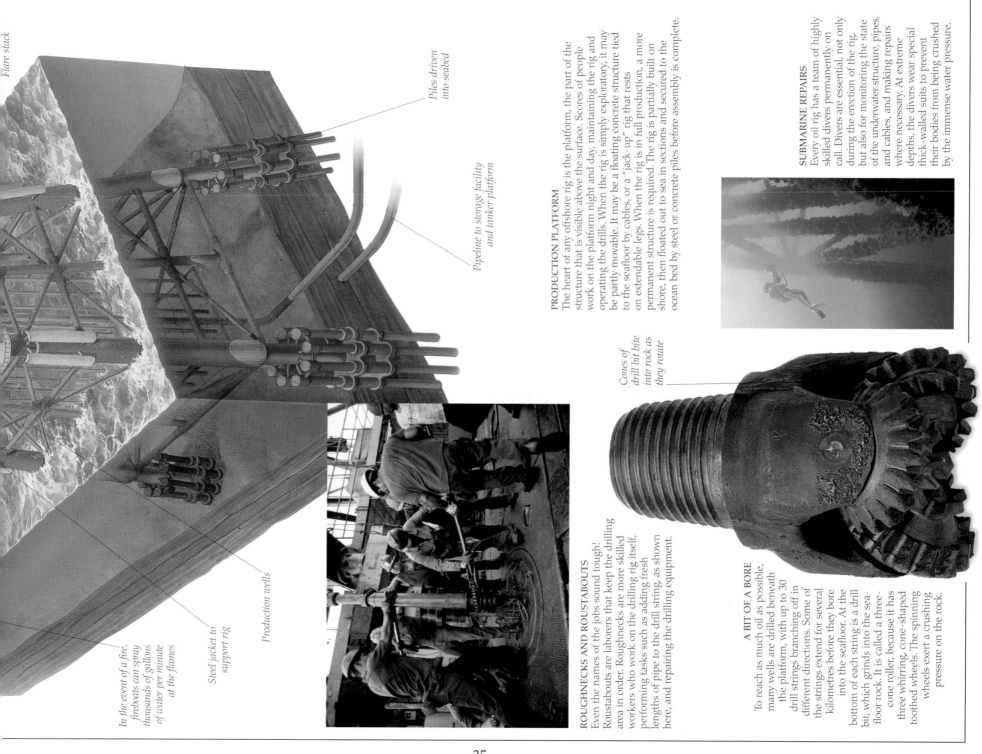

Flare stack

Piles driven into seabed

Pipeline to storage facility and tanker platform

In the event of a fire, fireboats can spray thousands of gallons of water per minute at the flames

Steel jacket to support rig

Production wells

PRODUCTION PLATFORM

The heart of any offshore rig is the platform, the part of the structure that is visible above the surface. Scores of people work on the platform night and day, maintaining the rig and operating the drills. When the rig is simply exploratory, it may be partly movable. It may be a floating concrete structure tied to the seafloor by cables, or a "jack-up" rig that rests on extendable legs. When the rig is in full production, a more permanent structure is required. The rig is partially built on shore, then floated out to sea in sections and secured to the ocean bed by steel or concrete piles before assembly is complete.

SUBMARINE REPAIRS

Every oil rig has a team of highly skilled divers permanently on call. Divers are essential, not only during the erection of the rig, but also for monitoring the state of the underwater structure, pipes, and cables, and making repairs where necessary. At extreme depths, the divers wear special thick-walled suits to prevent their bodies from being crushed by the immense water pressure.

Cones of drill bit bite into rock as they rotate

ROUGHNECKS AND ROUSTABOUTS

Even the names of the jobs sound tough! Roustabouts are laborers that keep the drilling area in order. Roughnecks are more skilled workers who work on the drilling rig itself, performing tasks such as adding fresh lengths of pipe to the drill string, as shown here, and repairing the drilling equipment.

A BIT OF A BORE

To reach as much oil as possible, many wells are drilled beneath the platform, with up to 30 drill strings branching off in different directions. Some of the strings extend for several kilometres before they bore into the seafloor. At the bottom of each string is a drill bit, which grinds into the sea-floor rock. It is called a three-cone roller, because it has three whirring, cone-shaped toothed wheels. The spinning wheels exert a crushing pressure on the rock.

Deepwater technology

THE FIRST OFFSHORE WELL out of the sight of land was drilled in 1947 in 15 feet of water. Just 30 years ago, deepwater operations meant exploring water depths up to 500 feet. Today, deepwater refers to a well in up to 5,000 feet of water, with ultra-deepwater exploratory drilling now occurring in water depths over 10,000 feet. A major new oil or gas floating production platform can cost billions of dollars and take up to three years to complete. Most of today's exploration is in frontier, deepwater, and ultra-deepwater areas. The challenges that have been overcome—and those that remain—in the exploitation of deepwater and ultra-deepwater reserves can be more daunting than the challenges of exploring space.

Photo: BP

Photo: Saudi Aramco

UNDERWATER ROBOTS (ROVS)

There has been an incredible evolution in the ability of people to work underwater from the diving "helmets" developed in the mid-16th century to today's underwater robots. "Remotely operated vehicles" (ROVs) repair and install the subsea systems. These underwater devices are similar to the rovers used in space exploration. Subsea ROVs are operated remotely by a worker on a nearby platform or vessel. An umbilical, or tether, carries power and command and control signals to the vehicle, and relays the status and sensory data back to the operator topside. ROVs can vary in size from small vehicles fitted with one TV camera to complex work systems that can have several dexterous manipulators, video cameras, mechanical tools, and other equipment. They are generally free flying, but some are bottom-founded on tracks.

Photo: Transocean

ALL ABOARD

At the heart of offshore exploration and production are the thousands of men and women working and living offshore. They generally work in one week or two weeks on and one or two-week off rotations. The workers are moved offshore and back by a fleet of modern helicopters. While offshore, these professionals generally work in 12-hour shifts, working the drilling rig or monitoring, testing, and adjusting the producing wells. Many offshore platforms contain all the comforts of a high-class hotel, including libraries, exercise facilities, movie theaters, medical facilities, and a host of other entertainment and health options. At least one North Sea platform has a chapter of the British bird watching society that actively catalogs and studies the numerous birds that use platforms as resting places during migration. In the Gulf of Mexico some offshore workers study the migratory habits of the Monarch butterfly, a regular offshore visitor during its migratory season.

ENGINEERING UNDERWATER

Deepwater oil and gas production platforms—indeed, all oil and gas production platforms—support the equipment necessary to separate the oil, gas, water, and solids that are produced from the wells. The platforms also are where the oil and gas is cleaned prior to transportation to a refinery or gas processing plant. Think of them as very large structures with small refineries atop. They are expensive to build, transport, and install. Much of the equipment for producing the oil and gas in deepwater is placed on the seabed. Subsea installations must withstand long-term exposure to seawater and extreme pressures over their lifespan of 20 years or more—safe and reliable operation are essential, and maintenance is costly and difficult. New technology is now available to process and separate the oil, gas, and water streams on the seafloor, thus avoiding the need for a processing platform. All of this subsea technology can be monitored and controlled in real time from an onshore facility. Getting the produced fluids from the seafloor to the shore requires an extensive network of pipelines and subsea boosting pumps, which have to pump the oil and gas for many miles.

FLOATING PRODUCTION VESSELS

Bringing oil from the deepwater to market is also a challenge. In addition to pipelines, floating production, storage, and offloading vessels (or FPSOs) can be used in deepwater where traditional platforms are not viable. FPSOs resemble giant oil tankers, but they are equipped with separation equipment like traditional platforms. The massive vessels can then hold the oil until shuttling tankers arrive to offload the product.

Graphic: ©Norsk Hydro

WORLD'S LARGEST CHRISTMAS TREE

Norway's most complicated and expensive offshore field, the Ormen Lange field, is being developed without any platforms. Instead, 24 subsea wells will pump the natural gas to a processing facility on the west coast of Norway before it is transported to the east coast of England by an almost 750-mile subsea export pipeline—the longest in the world. All the installations will be at sea depths of 2,500 to 3,400 feet. Ormen Lange will have a total of 14 underwater Christmas trees. An oil industry Christmas tree, originally called a crosstree, X-tree or XT, is a module that sits on top of the well head in an oil or gas well, which contains valves for testing and servicing, safety systems for shutting down, and an array of monitoring instruments. Weighing 65 tons, they are twice the size of other Christmas trees commonly used in offshore installations. Gas from the Ormen Lange field will be able to meet up to 20 percent of Britain's gas demand for up to 40 years

FINDING NEW SPECIES

Collaborating closely with key players in the oil and gas industry, the "Scientific and Environmental ROV Partnership using Existing iNdustrial Technology" (SERPENT) project aims to make cutting-edge ROV technology and drillships more accessible to the world's science community. So far, more than 20 new species have been identified and new behaviors of marine species have been observed.

Photo: SERPENT Project

GOING DEEPER

Deepwater oil exploration begins on the ocean surface with a fleet of seismic vessels. The boats use long cables to send energy impulses through the water and sea bottom where they reflect off the rocks below at different velocities. Recording and studying the reflections give geophysicists a picture of the rock formations below the surface. Seismic only identifies formations where hydrocarbons might be trapped—it does not find oil and gas. After the seismic has been analyzed and potential oil and gas-bearing formations identified, exploration drilling begins in order to determine what is in the target formations. New drilling ships and semi-submersible drilling rigs enable drillers to work at far greater depths than more conventional platforms that rest on the ocean floor. These ships use dynamic-positioning technology that continually accesses global positioning satellites to keep the vessel in the correct location.

Piped oil

IN THE EARLY DAYS OF THE OIL INDUSTRY, oil was carted laboriously away from oil wells in wooden barrels. The oil companies soon realized that the best way to move oil was to pump it through pipes. Today there are vast networks of pipelines around the world, both on land and under the sea. The US alone has about 190,000 miles (305,000 km) of oil pipes. The pipelines carry an array of different oil products, from gasoline to jet fuel, sometimes in "batches" within the same pipe separated by special plugs. Largest of all are the "trunk" pipelines that take crude oil from drilling regions to refineries or ports. Some are up to 48 in (122 cm) in diameter and over 1,000 miles (1,600 km) long. Trunk lines are fed by smaller "gathering" lines that carry oil from individual wells.

CLEVER PIGS
Every pipeline contains mobile plugs called pigs that travel along with the oil, either to separate batches of different oil products or to check for problems. The pigs get their name because early models made squealing noises as they moved through the pipes. A "smart" pig is a robot inspection unit with a sophisticated array of sensors. Propelled by the oil, the smart pig glides for hundreds of miles, monitoring every square inch of the pipe for defects such as corrosion.

Aerogel is such a good insulator that just a thin layer is enough to block the heat of this flame and stop the matches from igniting.

KEEPING IT WARM
If oil gets too cold, it becomes thicker and more difficult to pump through pipelines. Because of this, many pipes in colder parts of the world and under the sea are insulated with "aerogel." Created from a spongelike jelly of silica and carbon, aerogel is the world's lightest material, made of 99 percent air. All this air makes aerogel a remarkably good insulator.

THE POLITICS OF PIPELINE ROUTES
European nations wanted access to the Caspian Sea oil fields to increase their sources of supply for oil. So they backed the building of the Baku-Tbilisi–Ceyhan (BTC) pipeline. This runs 1,104 miles (1,776 km) from the Caspian Sea in Azerbaijan to the Mediterranean coast of Turkey via Georgia. Here the leaders of Georgia, Azerbaijan, and Turkey pose at the pipeline's completion in 2006.

PIPELINE CONSTRUCTION
Building an oil pipeline involves joining up tens of thousands of sections of steel piping. Each joint has to be expertly welded to prevent leakage. Construction is often relatively quick, since all the sections are prefabricated, but planning the pipeline's route and getting the agreement of all the people affected by it can take many years.

PIPELINES AND PEOPLE

Some pipelines are built through poor and environmentally sensitive regions, as seen here in Sumatra, Indonesia. Poor people living alongside the pipeline have no access to the riches carried by the pipe, but their lives can be disrupted by the construction—and any leaks once the pipeline is in operation. Vandalism of pipelines can cause dangerous situations as well.

This guard is protecting a pipeline in Saudi Arabia

OIL ON TAP

Completed in 1977, the Trans-Alaska Pipeline System (TAPS) stretches for over 800 miles (1,280 km) across Alaska. It carries crude oil from producer regions in the north to the port of Valdez in the south, from where the oil is shipped around the world. Arctic conditions and the need to cross mountain ranges and large rivers presented huge challenges to the construction engineers. Most US pipelines are subterranean, but much of the TAPS had to be built above ground because the soil in parts of Alaska is always frozen.

TERRORIST THREAT

Oil supplies carried by pipelines are so vital that they may become targets for terrorists, especially since many pass through politically unstable areas, such as parts of the Middle East. To guard against this threat, oil pipelines in some places are watched continuously by armed guards. However, many pipelines are too vast to patrol along their entire length.

QUAKE RISK

Scientists constantly monitor the ground for tremors along some parts of oil pipelines, since a strong earthquake could crack or break the pipes. This pipe was bent in a quake in Parkfield, California, which sits on the famous San Andreas Fault, where two plates of Earth's crust slide past one another.

Oil on the ocean

The tanker's small crew mostly lives and works in the deck house at the rear

Dᴀʏ ᴀɴᴅ ɴɪɢʜᴛ, some 3,500 oil tankers ply the world's oceans, transporting oil to wherever it is wanted. Mostly they transport crude oil, but sometimes they carry refined products, and these need special handling—bitumen, for example, must be heated to over 250°F (120°C) for loading. The quantity of oil moved by the tankers is vast. Each day, some 30 million barrels of oil are on the move. That's one-and-a-half times the daily consumption of oil in the entire US, and 15 times as much oil as is used in a day in the UK. To get a picture of just what a huge volume of liquid this is, imagine 2,000 Olympic swimming pools full to the brim with black oil. Modern double-hulled tanker designs and navigation systems mean that most of this oil is carried across the ocean safely. But every now and then there is an accident, and oil spills into the sea. Only a tiny fraction of all the oil transported is spilled, but the consequences can be devastating.

FIRST AFLOAT
Back in 1861, the American sailing ship *Elizabeth Watts* carried 240 kegs of oil from Philadelphia to England. But carrying such a flammable substance in wooden kegs in a wooden ship was a hazardous business. Then, in 1884, British shipbuilders custom-built the steel-hulled steamship *Glückauf* (right), which held the oil in a steel tank. This was the first modern oil tanker.

SUPERTANKER
The largest oil tankers, known as supertankers, are by far the world's biggest ships. They typically weigh over 330,000 tons (300,000 metric tons) empty and can carry millions of barrels of oil, worth hundreds of millions of dollars. Amazingly, these monster ships are so automated that they only need a crew of about 30. The vast size of supertankers means that they can take 6 miles (10 km) to stop, and need up to 2.5 miles (4 km) to turn. In the oil business, supertankers are called Ultra Large Crude Carriers (ULCCs). Very Large Crude Carriers (VLCCs) are not as large, but these tankers still weigh more than 220,000 tons (200,000 metric tons).

Supertanker   Tug boat   Ocean liner

GIANTS OF THE OCEAN
Supertankers are gigantic vessels, easily dwarfing the largest ocean liners. Some are even longer than the Empire State Building laid on its side. The largest of all is the *Knock Nevis* (once called the *Jahre Viking*). At 1,503 ft 5 in (458.4 m) long, it is the biggest ship ever to take to the ocean. The *Knock Nevis* weighs 600,500 tons (544,763 metric tons) empty, and 910,084 tons (825,614 metric tons) fully laden.

The interior of the hull is divided into several separate tanks to minimize the amount of oil lost if the hull is pierced

The bulk of the cargo of oil is carried below the waterline for stability

DOUBLE HULLS FOR DOUBLE SAFETY

All large new tankers are now required by law to have a double hull, with a second hull inside the outer hull to give extra security against oil leaks if the ship is damaged. The 6–10 ft (2–3 m) gap between the hulls can also be filled with water to make up for the vast drop in weight (and stability) when the tanker is sailing empty of oil.

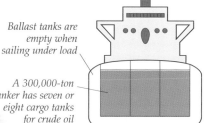

Ballast tanks are empty when sailing under load

A 300,000-ton tanker has seven or eight cargo tanks for crude oil

Sailing under load

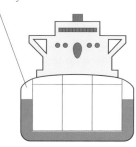

When sailing empty, the tanker takes on about 100,000 tons of seawater as ballast

Sailing empty

NATURAL SEEPS

Although we think of oil spills as caused by tankers, natural seepage is actually the largest single source of petroleum in the worldwide marine environment, contributing over 4 MMbbl/yr, or 47 percent of total inputs. Marine transportation is responsible for 33 percent of worldwide petroleum inputs, and only 3 percent of inputs in North American waters. Municipal and industrial waste accounts for 12 percent of worldwide petroleum inputs in the ocean, and 22 percent of petroleum inputs in North American marine waters.

OIL TERMINAL

After its long sea voyage, a tanker arrives at an oil terminal. Supertankers need water at least 65 ft (20 m) deep, so there is a limited number of suitable sites for oil terminals. The piers where the tankers moor are sometimes built so far out from the shore that dockers and crews have to drive to and from the ship. In the future, some terminals may be built as artificial "sea islands" in deep water, from which oil is piped ashore.

On-shore storage tanks

PUMPING OIL

To get oil off the tanker, long, articulated (jointed) arms swing into place. The arms are computer-controlled to enable them to hook up exactly with the oil outlet on the tanker's deck, known as the manifold. All the ship's oil tanks are connected to the manifold via valves and pipes. Once the arms are securely connected to the manifold, a pump called a deepwell cargo pump begins to pump the oil out.

Articulated-arm discharge system

Arm connects to manifold (oil outlet) on top of tanker

EXXON VALDEZ

The oil spill from the tanker Exxon Valdez off Alaska in 1989 one of the most publicized and studied environmental tragedies in history. The tanker hit a reef and about 11 million gallons (42 million liters) of oil leaked out and spread along 1,180 miles (1,900 km) of coastline. Almost two decades after the oil spill, some animal species injured by the spill have not fully recovered. In 1991, Exxon agreed to pay the United States and the State of Alaska $900 million over 10 years to restore the resources injured by the spill. Much has been accomplished over the years to prevent another *Exxon Valdez*-type accident. Today the ability of industry and government to respond is considerably strengthened from what it was in 1989.

Refining oil

To **turn it into usable forms**, crude oil is processed at an oil refinery. Here, crude oil is separated into different components to produce gasoline and hundreds of other products, from jet fuel to central heating oil. Refining involves a combination of "fractional distillation" and "cracking." Fractional distillation separates out the ingredients of oil into "fractions," such as light oil or heavy oil, using their different densities and boiling points. Cracking splits the fractions further into products such as gasoline by using heat and pressure to "crack" heavy, long-chain hydrocarbon molecules into shorter, lighter ones.

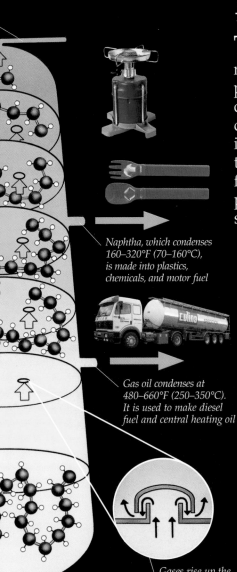

At 68°F (20°C) only four hydrocarbons remain. Methane and ethane are used to make chemicals. Propane and butane are bottled for portable gas stoves and lamps

Gasoline condenses at 70–106°F (20–70°C). It is mostly used as fuel for cars

Kerosene, which condenses at 320–480°F (160–250°C), can be used for jet fuel, heating, and lighting, and as a paint solvent

Mixture of crude oil gases at 750°F (400°C) passes into the pipe still

Naphtha, which condenses 160–320°F (70–160°C), is made into plastics, chemicals, and motor fuel

Gas oil condenses at 480–660°F (250–350°C). It is used to make diesel fuel and central heating oil

Gases rise up the tower via holes in the trays called bubble caps

SPLITTING BY FRACTIONS
Fractional distillation involves heating crude oil until it turns to vapor. The hot vapor is then fed into a pipe still—a tall tower divided at intervals by horizontal trays. The heaviest fractions cool quickly, condense to liquid, and settle at the bottom. Medium-weight fractions drift upward and condense on trays midway up the tower. The lightest fractions, including gasoline, rise right to the top before condensing.

The heaviest hydrocarbons condense as soon as they enter the column

STILL GOING
The temperature in a pipe still is carefully controlled. It gradually decreases with height, so that each tray is slightly cooler than the one below. Pipes exit the still at different levels to take away the different fractions as they condense or settle on the trays. Light fuels, such as propane, are removed at the top. The very heaviest fraction, the "residuum," is drawn off at the bottom. The pipes carry any fractions that need further processing on to the next refining stage.

OIL IN STORE
When crude oil arrives from the oil fields by pipeline or ship, it is stored in giant tanks ready for processing. Oil volume is usually measured in "barrels," with one barrel being equivalent to 35 gallons (159 liters). A typical large oil refinery can hold about 12 million barrels of crude oil in its tanks—enough to supply the whole of the US with oil for about three-quarters of a day.

FLEXICOKER

Early refineries were able to use only a small proportion of crude oil. Just one-quarter of each barrel, for example, could be turned into gasoline. Today, over half is made into gasoline, and most of the rest can be made into useful products, too. Flexicokers can convert previously wasted residuum into lighter products such as diesel. At the end of the process, an almost pure-carbon residue called coke is left, which is sold as solid fuel.

REFINERY COMPLEX

A typical refinery, like this one at Jubail in Saudi Arabia, is a gigantic complex of pipework and tanks covering an area the size of several hundred football fields. The pipe still is the large tower on the far left of the picture below. Big refineries operate around the clock, 365 days a year, employing some 1,000–2,000 people. The workers mostly regulate activities from inside control rooms. Outside, refineries are surprisingly quiet, with just the low hum of heavy machinery.

CRACKING TIME

Some fractions emerge from the pipe still ready for use. Others must be fed into bullet-shaped crackers like those above. While some gasoline is produced by pipe stills, most is made in crackers from heavy fractions using a process known as "cat cracking." This relies on intense heat (about 1,000°F/ 538°C) and the presence of a powder called a catalyst (the cat). The catalyst accelerates the chemical reactions that split up the hydrocarbons.

Energy and transportation

OIL IS THE WORLD'S top energy source, and over 80 percent of all the oil produced is used to provide energy to keep the world moving. Oil's energy is unlocked by burning it, which is why it can only ever be used once. A little is burned to provide heat for homes. A lot is burned to create steam to turn turbines and generate electricity. But most is burned in engines in the form of gas, diesel, maritime fuel oil, and aviation fuel for transportation. It takes 30 million barrels of oil each day to keep all our cars and trucks, trains, ships, and aircraft on the move.

Reva G-Wiz electric car

The G-Wiz has a range of 40 miles(64 km) and a top speed of about 40 mph (64 kph)

A RANGE OF USES
Oil-burners revolutionized heating in the home when they were introduced in the 1920s. Before then, heat came from open, smoky fires that needed constant attention and big stores of coal or wood. Oil-burning ranges like the one above combined cooking with heating. They could also be used to provide hot water.

WHAT COMES FROM A BARREL OF OIL

Lubricants 0.9%
Other refined products 1.5%
Asphalt & Road Oil 1.7%
Liquified Refinery Gas 2.8%
Residual Fuel Oil 3.3%
Marketable Coke 5.0%
Still Gas 5.4%
Jet Fuel 12.3%

Distillate Fuel Oil 15.3%

Gasoline 51.4%

Source: California Energy Commission.

2. Rising piston compresses the fuel in the cylinder

3. Spark plug ignites the fuel, which gives off hot gases as it burns

4. Hot gases expand, forcing down the piston and turning the crankshaft

TWO ENGINES IN ONE
To reduce fuel use and pollution, car makers have introduced "hybrid" cars that have both a gas engine and an electric motor. The engine starts the car and charges a battery. The battery then powers an electric motor, which takes over from the engine. Some cars are entirely battery-powered. The Reva G-Wiz, shown here, can be charged by plugging it into a socket at home.

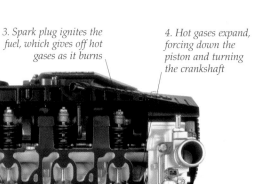

1. Fuel inlet valve lets air and fuel enter the cylinder

Cylinders fire at different times to keep the crankshaft turning

Belts drive a fan and a water pump to cool the engine

BURNING INSIDE
Most cars are powered by internal combustion engines, so named because they burn gas inside. Gas vapor is fed into each of the engine's cylinders and then squeezed, or compressed, by a rising piston. Squeezing makes the vapor so warm that it is easily ignited by an electrical spark. The vapor burns rapidly and expands, thrusting the piston back down. As each piston descends, it drives a crankshaft around, which turns the car's wheels via shafts and gears.

OIL-SHAPED LIVES

Fueled by oil, the car has allowed cities to spread out as never before, with sprawling suburbs like this. The houses can be spacious and yards big, but the downside is that stores and workplaces may be so far away that it is difficult to live in suburbia without a car.

Most suburbs do not have public transportation

F1 cars typically only travel 2 miles per gallon (0.4 km per liter of fuel), so they have to make pit stops during a race to refuel

RACING OIL

By varying the proportions of the different hydrocarbons and adding extra components, oil companies can tailor fuel to suit different engines. Racing regulations ensure that Formula One cars use a fuel similar to that used by production cars, but it is a volatile version that gives high performance. Racing fuel is hugely uneconomical and places too much stress on the engine for everyday use.

HEAVY HAULAGE

Most cars run on gas. Trucks and buses, however, run mostly on thicker diesel oil. Diesel engines do not need a spark. Instead, the pistons compress the air in the cylinders so hard and warm it so much that when diesel fuel is squirted into the cylinders it ignites instantly. Diesel engines burn less oil than gas engines and are cheaper to run, but they have to be heavier and more robust to take the extra compression. This makes them slower to speed up than gas engines, which is why they are less popular for cars.

FUEL FOR FLYING

About three-quarters of all the oil used for transportation is burned by road vehicles, but an increasing proportion is consumed by aircraft. A large airliner can burn more than 20,000 gallons (77,000 liters) of jet fuel on a flight from Washington, D.C., to San Francisco. Jet fuel is slightly different from gas, having a higher "flash point" (ignition temperature). This makes jet fuel much safer to transport than gas.

Fuel is stored in tanks in the wings

Materials from oil

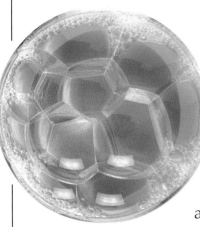

OIL IS NOT JUST A SOURCE OF ENERGY—it is also a remarkable raw material. Its rich mix of hydrocarbons can be processed to give useful substances known as petrochemicals. Processing usually alters the hydrocarbons so completely that it is hard to recognize the oil origins of petrochemical products. An amazing range of materials and objects can be made from petrochemicals, from plastics to perfumes and bed sheets. We use many oil products as synthetic alternatives to natural materials, including synthetic rubbers instead of natural rubber, and detergents instead of soap. But oil also gives us entirely new, unique materials such as nylon.

COMING CLEAN
Most detergents are based on petrochemicals. Water alone will not remove greasy dirt from surfaces, since it is repelled by oil and grease. Detergents work because they contain chemicals called surface active agents, or surfactants, which are attracted to both grease and water. They cling to dirt and loosen it, so that it can be removed during washing.

Oil in lipstick acts as a lubricant

Lipstick

LOOKING GOOD
Lipstick, eyeliner, mascara, moisturizer, and hair dye are just some of the many beauty products that are based on petrochemicals. For example, most skin lotions use petroleum jelly— a waxy, kerosenelike material made from oil—as a key ingredient. Some brands advertise their lines as "petroleum-free" if, unusually, they do not contain oil products.

Eyeliner

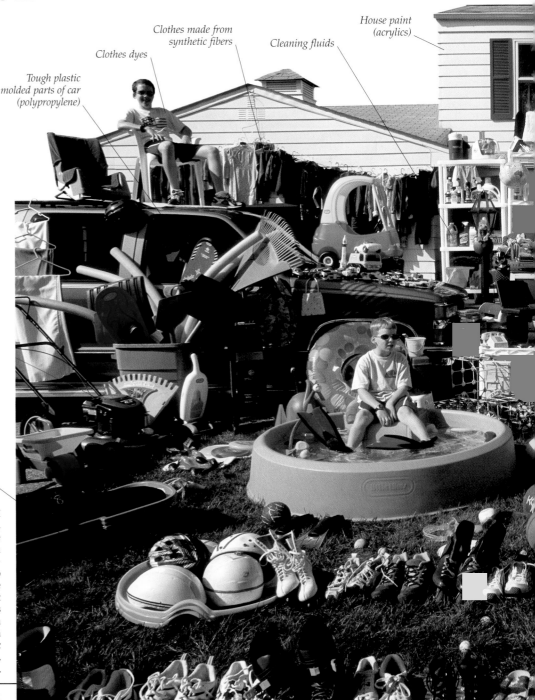

Clothes dyes

Tough plastic molded parts of car (polypropylene)

Clothes made from synthetic fibers

Cleaning fluids

House paint (acrylics)

Grass grown with the aid of fertilizers made from petrochemicals

LIVING WITH PETROLEUM
To show just how many ways we use oil, this American family was asked to pose outside their home with all the things in their house that are made from oil-based materials. In fact, they had to almost empty their home, since there were remarkably few things that did not involve oil. In addition to countless plastic objects, there were drugs from the bathroom, cleaning materials from the kitchen, clothes made from synthetic fibers, cosmetics, glues, clothes dyes, footwear, and much more.

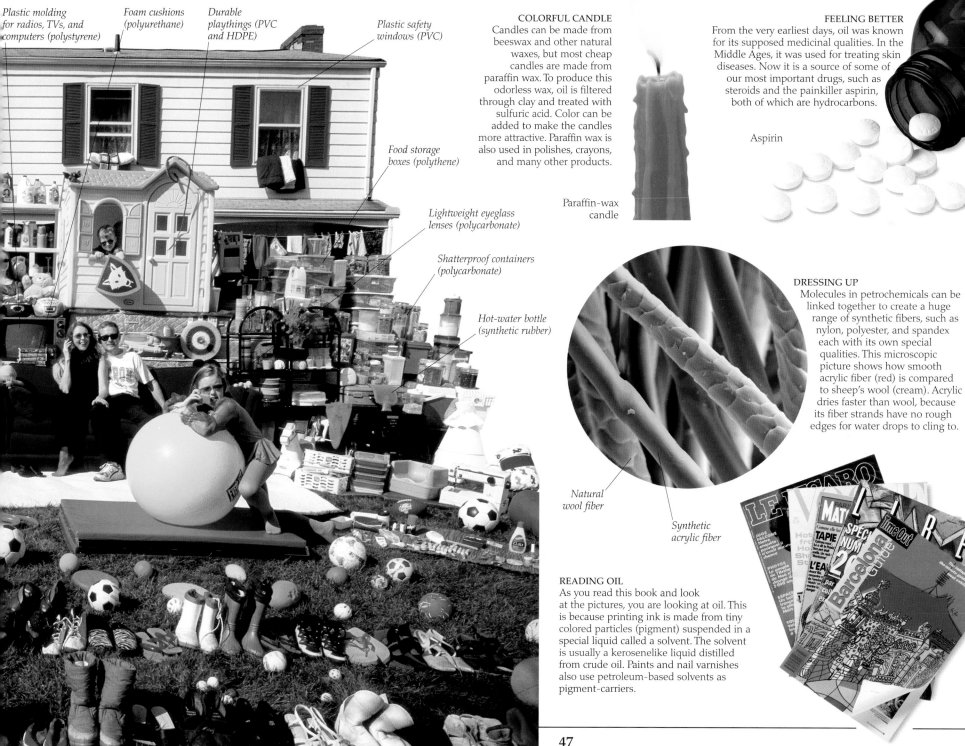

Plastic molding for radios, TVs, and computers (polystyrene)

Foam cushions (polyurethane)

Durable playthings (PVC and HDPE)

Plastic safety windows (PVC)

Food storage boxes (polythene)

Lightweight eyeglass lenses (polycarbonate)

Shatterproof containers (polycarbonate)

Hot-water bottle (synthetic rubber)

COLORFUL CANDLE
Candles can be made from beeswax and other natural waxes, but most cheap candles are made from paraffin wax. To produce this odorless wax, oil is filtered through clay and treated with sulfuric acid. Color can be added to make the candles more attractive. Paraffin wax is also used in polishes, crayons, and many other products.

Paraffin-wax candle

FEELING BETTER
From the very earliest days, oil was known for its supposed medicinal qualities. In the Middle Ages, it was used for treating skin diseases. Now it is a source of some of our most important drugs, such as steroids and the painkiller aspirin, both of which are hydrocarbons.

Aspirin

DRESSING UP
Molecules in petrochemicals can be linked together to create a huge range of synthetic fibers, such as nylon, polyester, and spandex each with its own special qualities. This microscopic picture shows how smooth acrylic fiber (red) is compared to sheep's wool (cream). Acrylic dries faster than wool, because its fiber strands have no rough edges for water drops to cling to.

Natural wool fiber

Synthetic acrylic fiber

READING OIL
As you read this book and look at the pictures, you are looking at oil. This is because printing ink is made from tiny colored particles (pigment) suspended in a special liquid called a solvent. The solvent is usually a kerosenelike liquid distilled from crude oil. Paints and nail varnishes also use petroleum-based solvents as pigment-carriers.

Plastics and polymers

Each ethene monomer in the chain has two hydrogen atoms (white) and two carbon atoms (black)

Polyethylene polymer

PLASTICS PLAY an incredibly important part in the modern world. They find their way into our homes in many different ways and forms, from boxes used to keep food fresh to TV remote controls. Plastics are essentially materials that can be heated and molded into almost any shape. They have this quality because they are made from incredibly long, chainlike molecules called polymers. Some plastic polymers are entirely natural, such as horn and amber. But nearly all the polymers we use today are artificially made, and the majority of them are produced from oil and natural gas. Scientists are able to use the hydrocarbons in oil to create an increasing variety of polymers—not only for plastics, but also to make synthetic fibers and other materials.

18th-century tortoiseshell snuff box

NATURAL POLYMERS
In the past, people made buttons, handles, combs, and boxes from natural polymers such as shellac (secretions of the lac insect) and tortoiseshell (mostly the shells of hawksbill turtles). A tortoiseshell box like this was made by heating and melting the tortoiseshell, and then letting it cool and solidify in a mold.

MAKING POLYMERS
Polymers are long-chain molecules made up of smaller molecules called monomers. Polyethylene, for example, is a plastic polymer made from 50,000 molecules of a simple hydrocarbon monomer called ethene. Scientists make the ethene monomers join together in a chemical reaction known as polymerization. Worldwide, over 60 million tons of polyethylene are produced each year.

Bakelite telephone

EARLY PLASTIC
The first semisynthetic plastic, called Parkesine, was created by Alexander Parkes (1813–90) in 1861. It was made by modifying cellulose, the natural polymer found in cotton. The age of modern plastics began in 1907, when Leo Baekeland (1863–1944) discovered how to make new polymers using chemical reactions. His revolutionary polymer, called Bakelite, was made by reacting phenol and formaldehyde under heat and pressure. Bakelite had many uses, from aircraft propellers to jewelry and door knobs, but its greatest success was as a casing for electrical goods, since it was an excellent electrical insulator.

POLYETHYLENE
Tough yet soft and flexible, polyethylene is one of the most versatile and widely used of all plastics. First made by the ICI company in 1933, it is also one of the oldest plastics. Most plastic soda bottles are made of polyethylene.

HDPE
There are many kinds of polyethylene, including HDPE (high density polyethylene). HDPE is an especially tough, dense form of polyethylene that is often used to make toys, cups, detergent bottles, and garbage cans.

LDPE
In LDPE (low density polyethylene), the polymers are only loosely packed, making a very light, very flexible plastic. Clear LDPE film is widely used for packaging bread and as a kitchen food-wrap.

PVC
PVC (polyvinyl chloride), one of the hardest plastics, is used for sewer pipes and window frames. When softened by substances called plasticizers, it can be used to make shoes, shampoo bottles, medical blood bags, and much more.

POLYPROPYLENE
A rugged plastic that resists most solvents and acids, polypropylene is often used for medicine and industrial chemical bottles. Photographic film is also made of polypropylene, as the plastic is not harmed by the chemicals used in the developing process.

POLYSTYRENE
When molded hard and clear, polystyrene is used to make items such as CD cases. Filled with tiny gas bubbles, it forms the light foam used to package eggs. This foam is also used for disposable coffee cups, because it is a good heat insulator.

Not all hydrocarbon polymers are plastics. The polymers can also be strung together to make light, strong fibers. Synthetic polymer fibers are used not only use to make everyday clothes, but also to produce special items of sportswear. Based on studies of shark skin, this Fastskin® swimsuit is designed to let the swimmer glide through the water with the least resistance.

Aramid fibers

Kevlar® bullet-proof vest

TOUGH THREADS

In 1961, DuPont™ chemist Stephanie Kwolek (b. 1923) discovered how to spin solid fibers from liquid chemicals including hydrocarbons. The resulting fibers, called aramid fibers, are amazingly tough. Aramid fibers such as Kevlar® can be woven together to make a material that is light enough to wear as a jacket, yet tough enough to stop a bullet.

CARBON POWER

By embedding fibers of carbon in them, plastics such as polyester can be turned into an incredibly strong, light material called carbon-fiber reinforced plastic (CFRP or CRP). Because it combines plastic and carbon, CRP is described as a composite material. It is ideal for use where high strength and lightness need to be combined, as in the artificial limbs of this sprinter.

CRP is as tough as metal, but can be molded into any shape

SOCCER BUBBLE

Plastic polymers do not have to be hydrocarbons made from oil or natural gas. In fluorocarbon polymers such as Teflon® (used to coat nonstick cooking pans) and ethylene tetrafluoroethylene (ETFE), it is not hydrogen but fluorine that links up with carbon. ETFE can be made into tough, semitransparent sheets, like those shown here covering the futuristic Allianz Stadium in Munich, Germany. The stadium glows red when the Bayern Munich soccer team plays at home.

POLYCARBONATE

Being hard to break and capable of withstanding very high temperatures, polycarbonate is becoming increasingly popular in manufacturing. DVDs, MP3 players, electric light covers, and sunglass lenses are all typically made with polycarbonate.

COMMON PLASTICS

Hydrocarbons can be linked together in different ways to form hundreds of different types of plastic polymer, each with its own special quality. When polymer strands are held rigidly together, for example, the plastic is stiff like polycarbonate. When the strands can slip easily over one another, the plastic is bendable like polyethylene. So the makers of plastic items can select a plastic that gives just the right qualities for the intended use.

Global oil

MOTORING BEGINS AT CARLSON'S ESSO STATION INTERSECTION OF 130 & 40 2 MILES FROM PENNSVILLE FERRY COMPLETE LUBRICATION ME UP TEL PENNSGROVE 912 DEEPWATER N.J.

THE FIRST OIL GIANT
Standard Oil began as a small oil refining company in Cleveland, Ohio, but it quickly grew into the first giant oil company and made the fortunes of Rockefeller and Harkness. In the 1920s and 30s, the company became famous throughout the developed world as Esso, and Esso gas stations like this one in New Jersey became a familiar sight. Now called ExxonMobile, it is the biggest of the investor-owned giant oil companies.

The Emirates Tower is one of the world's tallest buildings

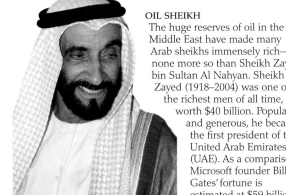

OIL SHEIKH
The huge reserves of oil in the Middle East have made many Arab sheikhs immensely rich—none more so than Sheikh Zayed bin Sultan Al Nahyan. Sheikh Zayed (1918–2004) was one of the richest men of all time, worth $40 billion. Popular and generous, he became the first president of the United Arab Emirates (UAE). As a comparison, Microsoft founder Bill Gates' fortune is estimated at $59 billion.

OIL HAS MADE INDIVIDUALS WEALTHY, brought huge profits to companies, and transformed poor countries into rich ones. Right from the early days of oil in the 19th century, oil barons made fortunes almost overnight. In Baku, there was Hadji Taghiyev (1823–1924). In the US, the first oil millionaire was Jonathan Watson (1819–94) of Titusville, Pennsylvania, where Drake drilled the first US oil well (p. 12). Then came the great oil dynasties of John D. Rockefeller (1839–1937) and Edward Harkness (1874–1940), and later the Texas oil millionaires such as Haroldson Hunt (1889–1974) and Jean Paul Getty (1892–1976)—each acclaimed at one time as the richest man in the world. In the late 20th century, it was Arab sheikhs who were famous for their oil wealth. Now it is Russia's turn.

OIL PROSPERITY
Oil wealth has transformed countries such as Saudi Arabia, UAE, and other states along the Persian Gulf. Half a century ago, these were largely poor countries where desert nomads lived simply, as they had done for thousands of years. The economies of these countries are now booming, and gleaming modern cities like Dubai City in the UAE are rising amid the sands.

World's 10 largest oil and gas companies

1. Saudi Aramco (Saudi Arabia)
2. National Iranian Oil Company (Iran)
3. Gazprom (Russia – partially state-owned)
4. Qatar Petroleum (Qatar)
5. Kuwait Petroleum Co. (Kuwait)
6. Petroleos de Venezuela (Venezuela)
7. Adnoc (UAE)
8. Nigerian Nacional Petroleum Co. (Nigeria)
9. Sonatrach (Algeria)
10. Libya NOC (Libya)

WHO IS THE LARGEST?

Wal-Mart has displaced ExxonMobil as the largest corporation on the global Fortune 500 list. ExxonMobil is the largest and most profitable investor-owned oil company, but it is not the largest oil company in the world. The largest company by a large margin is Saudi Aramco, which has 260 billion barrels of oil and natural gas reserves, compared with 23 billion for ExxonMobil, making it No. 12. In fact, all of the world's 10 largest oil and natural gas companies are government-controlled companies, called national oil companies (NOCs).

Chelsea player, Michael Ballack

RUSSIAN RICHES

When the Soviet Union broke up in the 1990s, many state oil and gas companies were sold off cheaply. Astute Russian investors, such as Mikhail Khodorkovsky and Roman Abramovich, bought into them and became billionaires. Abramovich used his wealth to buy London's Chelsea soccer team, making him a celebrity and the club successful.

OIL CONNECTS THE WORLD

The world's airlines offered nearly 2.4 million scheduled flights per month in 2007–that is 100,000 more than in January, 2006, and 300,000 more than in January, 2002. International routes between Western Europe and the Middle East increased the most. Airplane makers are researching biofuels for planes, but it's a difficult task because biofuels do not pack the same energy punch that fossil fuels do. An aviation fuel also must remain liquid at the low temperatures that surround an aircraft in flight and biofuels tend to solidify more quickly than their petroleum-derived equivalent.

BP solar cells in the Philippines

In 2000 BP changed its logo to a flower symbol

Waste gas from oil production is burned off or flared

CURSE OF RESOURCES

The "resource curse" refers to the paradox that countries with an abundance of natural resources tend to have less economic growth than countries without these natural resources. Governments do not always ensure that everyone benefits from the riches brought by oil. For example, in oil-rich Nigeria, poor local Urohobo people in the Niger Delta bake krokpo-garri (tapioca) in the heat of a gas flare, which can cause health problems. Nigeria and other countries are working to reduce flaring, but lack of access to energy is a problem for the world's poor. World agencies report that the health of the poor is damaged because they lack access to clean energy, like electricity, and face exposure to smoke from open fires.

GOING GREEN

Environmental concerns have hurt the image of oil as a fuel. The oil industry has made many improvements that have reduced its environmental impact, and is making major investments in alternative energy. BP, for example, now has a large share of the solar power market. It has been part of the world's biggest ever solar energy program, which provides solar power for isolated villages in the Philippines.

Oil and power

OIL IS SO CENTRAL to the modern way of life that countries have gone to war over it. Oil is crucial to the prosperity of a nation, providing energy to fuel everything from its transportation networks to its industries. It can also be vital to a nation's survival, since many of the military machines that protect it run on oil. So it is not surprising that oil was at the heart of many conflicts in the 20th century, and plays a key part today in many confrontations. The enormous oil reserves of Middle Eastern countries such as Iran and Iraq have kept them in the forefront of global news and guaranteed the world's continuing interest in their affairs. Now the exploitation of reserves in Russia, Venezuela, Nigeria, and other countries is making the politics of oil even more complex.

FUELING THE NAVY
Oil giant BP began as the Anglo-Persian Oil Company, founded after oil was discovered in Iran in 1908. This was the first big oil company to use Middle Eastern oil. Its oil was vital to Britain in World War I (1914–18). Churchill's (at that time, First Lord of the Admiralty) insistence that the British navy convert from coal to oil marks the beginning of the modern oil age. Most other navies converted shortly after the war and the world's navies became the largest early users of oil as fuel.

Gasoline

THE FIRES OF WAR
Oil has played a key role in the wars that have rocked the Persian Gulf region over the last 20 years. When Iraqi dictator Saddam Hussein's troops invaded Kuwait in 1990, he claimed that Kuwait had been drilling into Iraqi oil fields. And when the US and its allies intervened to liberate Kuwait, they were partly motivated by the need to secure oil supplies. The retreating Iraqis set fire to Kuwaiti oil wells (right).

THE OIL CRISIS
In 1973, war broke out between Israel and Arab forces led by Syria and Egypt. OPEC halted all oil exports to Israel's supporters, including the US and many European nations. This led to severe oil shortages in the West, which had long relied on Middle Eastern oil, and long lines for gasoline. US gasoline stations sold fuel to drivers with odd- and even-numbered plates on alternate days.

Sheikh Yamani was famed for his shrewd negotiating skills

OIL LEADER
In the 1960s, the key oil-producing nations, including those of the Middle East, formed OPEC (Organization of Petroleum Exporting Countries) to represent their interests. Saudi Arabia's Sheikh Yamani (b. 1930) was a leading OPEC figure for 25 years. He is best known for his role in the 1973 oil crisis, when he persuaded OPEC to quadruple oil prices.

MOSSY'S DOWNFALL
Mohammed Mossadegh (1882–1967) was the popular, democratically elected prime minister of Iran from 1951 to 1953. He was removed from power in a coup supported by the US and Great Britain after he nationalized the assets of the British-controlled Anglo-Iranian (formerly Persian) Oil Company.

Skyscrapers along the Sheikh Zahid in Dubai.

OIL AND WAR WORLD II

The leaders of World War II, on both sides, knew that an army's lifeblood was petroleum. Before the War, experts had dismissed Adolph Hitler's idea that he could conquer the world largely because Germany had almost no local supplies of petroleum. Hitler, however, had assembled a large industrial complex to manufacture synthetic petroleum from Germany's abundant coal supplies. Oil become a strategy of war, as the Allied forces conducted a bombing campaign on German's synthetic fuels industry, paralyzing major parts of the German war offensive. A lack of oil also slowed Japan's war machine.

A German 1930s Junker 52 airplane

RISE OF NATIONAL OIL COMPANIES

A national oil company (NOC) is a government-owned company that operates the country's oil and gas resources. The largest NOCs operate in Saudi Arabia, Iran, Kuwait, UAE, and Venezuela, but NOCs also operate in Norway, Malaysia, India, and Mexico. Today, NOCs control three-quarters of the world's oil reserves. The NOCs have become sophisticated, extremely capable, and profitable business entities in their own right, providing both financial strength and prestige for their countries. For example, Venezuela's desire to exercise more control over its resources has meant a smaller role for international oil companies in that country.

MODERN DUBAI

Since the discovery of oil more than 30 years ago, the United Arab Emirates (UAE) has undergone a profound transformation from a region of small desert principalities to a modern state with a high standard of living. As the center of trade and tourism, Dubai has grown in prominence—its prosperity is shown in its mega-shopping malls and luxury resorts on a turquoise sea, which attract around seven million tourists a year. Dubai's growth rate surpasses even China, which also has one of the fastest growing economies in the world.

CHINA'S THIRST FOR OIL

Energy fuels economies. China's thirst for oil and other resources impacts its foreign policy and its relationships with other countries. China's need for oil is much greater than its own proven oil reserves, which has caused it to acquire interests in exploration and production in Kazakhstan, Russia, Venezuela, Sudan, West Africa, Iran, Saudi Arabia, and Canada. China currently imports 32 percent of its oil and is expected to double its need for imported oil by 2010.

The Kuwait oil fires in 1991 started by Iraqi troops burned for seven months and consumed a billion barrels of oil.

Oil and the environment

While the world relies on oil and gas for most of its energy and is likely to do so for years to come, there is growing concern that the global climate is warming and that carbon dioxide (CO_2) emissions from human activity play a role. Climate change concerns could lead to curbing carbon emissions, which will require changes in energy production as well as changes in the way individuals and industrial companies use energy. Petroleum industry practices have changed a lot in the past 50 years, and many rigorous controls and technological innovations have been implemented to take better care of the natural environment. The US oil and natural gas industry has made investments of $148 billion in improving its environmental performance since 1990—$504 for every man, woman, and child in the United States. The results are seen in smaller "footprints" (the amount of surface area disturbed), less waste generated, cleaner and safer operations, and greater compatibility with the environment.

WATERING PLANTS
Pistachios and many other food crops in California are grown with water brought to the surface with oil and gas production. Water from coalbed methane production in Wyoming is being tested for watering barley and other crops. New techniques for cleaning the contaminants in water produced during oil and gas operations significantly improve water quality for surface discharge, injection or beneficial use.

Sun

Solar radiation warms Earth

Greenhouse gases surrounding Earth

Some infrared radiation reemitted by the ground escapes into space

Some infrared radiation is trapped by greenhouse gases, making Earth warmer

HURRICANE SAFETY
In 2005, just before Hurricanes Katrina and Rita roared through the Gulf of Mexico, all offshore production platforms were evacuated to protect workers and production was shutdown. As a result there were no lost lives and no significant offshore spills. There are over 4,000 platforms in the Gulf of Mexico, which means that more than 97 percent of the platforms survived these record-breaking storms. Offshore facilities built since 1988 are designed to withstand "100-year storms," a designation that includes everything up to Category 5 events.

THE GREENHOUSE EFFECT
Solar radiation warms up the ground, which then re-emits infrared radiation back into the atmosphere. Much of this escapes into space, but some is trapped by certain gases in the atmosphere, such as carbon dioxide, water vapor, and methane, which act like the glass in a greenhouse. This "greenhouse effect" keeps Earth warm enough to sustain life. Extra carbon dioxide in the atmosphere is perhaps trapping too much infrared radiation, making the world warmer. Carbon dioxide is emitted from power plants that burn fossil fuels, primarily coal, from auto emissions, and buildings. Deforestation is the second principle cause of atmospheric carbon dioxide. Deforestation is responsible for 25 percent of all carbon emissions entering the atmosphere by the burning and cutting of about 34 million acres of trees each year. Methane, the second most important greenhouse gas, is emitted primarily from agriculture, such as rice paddies and cow flatulence, and from fossil fuel production.

SMALL FOOTPRINTS
In the past 30 years, production facility footprints have shrunk dramatically. The size of drilling pads has been reduced by up to 80 percent. If Prudhoe Bay oil field in Alaska were opened with today's technology, its footprint would be almost a third of its current size. New seismic and remote sensing technologies, including satellite and aerial surveying, now boost the likelihood that an oil or gas well will be successful and there will be fewer dry holes to disturb the environment. Advanced directional drilling allows access to an underground target the size of a closet more than 5 miles from the drilling rig, making it possible to drill multiple wells from a single location.

GLOBAL CHANGES

Although the US was the largest CO_2 emitter from energy use 2005, most projected growth of CO_2 emissions is from developing countries. Reducing CO_2 emissions would require global, broad-based actions over decades. These actions include boosting energy efficiency and reducing demand, increasing use of alternate energy sources that are not carbon based (wind, solar, tidal, geothermal), shifting to renewable fuels like ethanol, and carbon capture and storage methods.

CAPTURING CARBON

Coal can be converted into a clean-burning gas and the carbon dioxide can be captured and injected deep underground into empty oil and gas reservoirs to dramatically reduce air pollution from coal. Burning coal is the largest source of carbon dioxide emissions from energy production. The oil and gas industry is responsible for oil and gas fields that are the geological structures with the greatest potentials for carbonsequestration, and in some cases the CO_2 can be used to get more oil out of existing reservoirs.

REDUCED EMISSIONS

Since the 1970s, cleaner-burning gasoline and more efficient engines have produced a 41 percent reduction in vehicle emissions. That is in spite of a substantial increase in the number of drivers and the number of miles traveled.

Emissions from 33 cars made today are equal to one car built in the 1960s.

ULTRA-LOW SULFUR DIESEL

Ultra Low Sulfur Diesel (ULSD) fuel is a cleaner-burning diesel fuel that enables the use of cleaner technology diesel engines and vehicles, resulting in significantly improved air quality. Annual emission reductions will be equivalent to removing the pollution from more than 90 percent of today's trucks and buses, when the current heavy-duty vehicle fleet has been completely replaced in 2030.

RIGS TO REEFS

When the oil in a well is gone, the well must be plugged below ground, making it hard to determine it was ever there. The platforms may be removed for recycling or appropriate disposal, or they may be relocated for beneficial use as artificial reefs. Within six months to a year after a rig is toppled, it becomes covered with barnacles, coral, sponges, clams, and other sea creatures. The artificial reefs expand valuable fish habitats in areas lacking natural reefs, such as the Gulf of Mexico and Thailand—more than 120 platforms in the Gulf of Mexico have been converted to artificial reefs designed to enhance fish habitat and create areas for recreational fishing.

INVISIBLE ROADS

In the Arctic, companies build ice roads and ice drilling pads to conduct their operations. These structures melt away in the spring, leaving no sign that they ever existed.

Demand and consumption

THE WORLD CURRENTLY USES about 86 million barrels per day of oil—40,000 gallons every second. And the world's energy needs continue to climb as economies and populations expand, especially in the developing countries. Over 80 percent of the world's population is expected to live in developing countries by 2030. At the same time, oil and gas production in the US and Europe is declining. Oil and natural gas resources are increasingly concentrated in developing countries. The International Energy Agency projects that the increase in energy demand will require $20 trillion in investment over the next 25 years—$3,000 for every person alive today. Over half the amount is for electricity generation and distribution. The challenge is to produce the clean, affordable and abundant energy resources needed to run our world.

Country	Reserves
Saudi Arabia	264.3 billion barrels
Canada	178.8 billion
Iran	132.5 billion
Iraq	115 billion
Kuwait	101.5 billion
United Arab Emirates	97.8 billion
Venezuela	79.7 billion
Russia	60 billion
Libya	39.1 billion
Nigeria	35.9 billion

Offshore rigs extract oil from reserves deep under the seabed

Saudi Arabia 12.9%

Russia 12.1%

NEW OIL RESERVES

With growing demand for energy worldwide, the challenge has become how to provide the adequate, affordable and reliable supply of energy needed to grow the global economy while protecting the natural environment. The U.S. Geological Survey estimates that the ultimate recoverable resources of conventional oil, including natural gas liquids, at more than 3.3 trillion barrels. Of these, less than a third have been consumed to date, with almost 2.4 trillion barrels yet to be produced. In addition, there are also vast resources of "non-conventional" oil - some 7 trillion barrels initially in place that will require technology advances to access.

OIL RESERVES BY COUNTRY (2006)

The world's biggest subterranean oil reserves are in Saudi Arabia, whose Ghawar field is the world's largest oil field. Measuring over 174 miles by 19 miles (280 km by 30 km), the massive Ghawar field produces over 6 percent of all the world's oil. Much of the rest of the world's oil is also underground in the Middle East. Canada has reserves that are almost as large as Saudi Arabia's, but most are in the form of oil sands, from which oil is difficult to extract.

 = approximately 20 billion barrels

US
20.5 million barrels per day

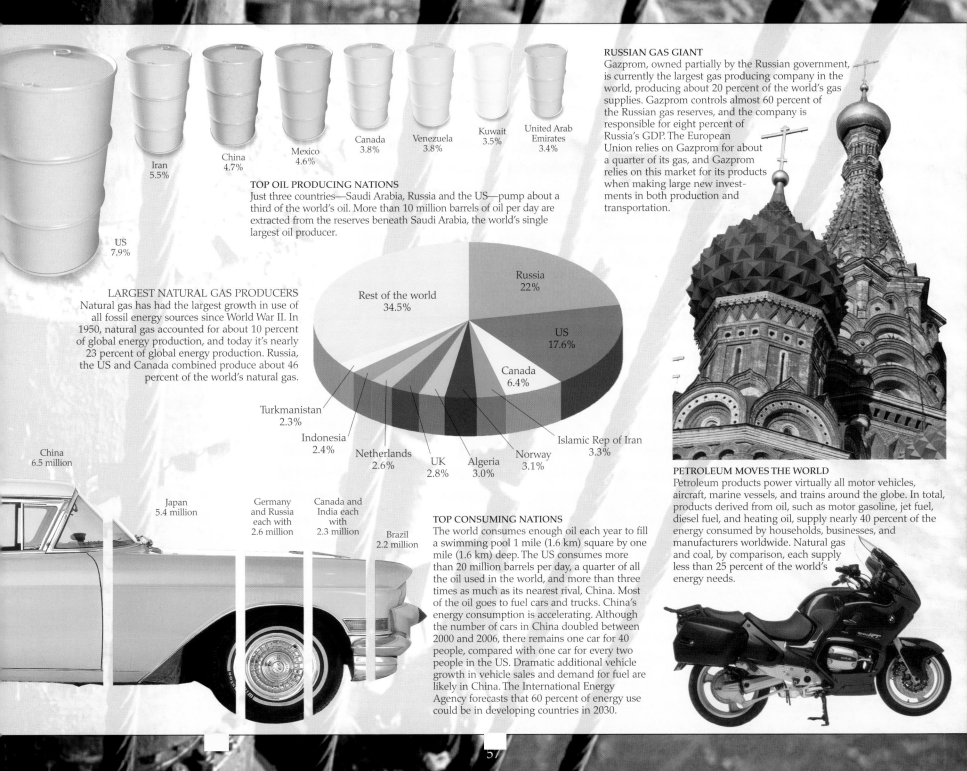

Iran
5.5%

China
4.7%

Mexico
4.6%

Canada
3.8%

Venezuela
3.8%

Kuwait
3.5%

United Arab
Emirates
3.4%

US
7.9%

RUSSIAN GAS GIANT
Gazprom, owned partially by the Russian government, is currently the largest gas producing company in the world, producing about 20 percent of the world's gas supplies. Gazprom controls almost 60 percent of the Russian gas reserves, and the company is responsible for eight percent of Russia's GDP. The European Union relies on Gazprom for about a quarter of its gas, and Gazprom relies on this market for its products when making large new investments in both production and transportation.

TOP OIL PRODUCING NATIONS
Just three countries—Saudi Arabia, Russia and the US—pump about a third of the world's oil. More than 10 million barrels of oil per day are extracted from the reserves beneath Saudi Arabia, the world's single largest oil producer.

LARGEST NATURAL GAS PRODUCERS
Natural gas has had the largest growth in use of all fossil energy sources since World War II. In 1950, natural gas accounted for about 10 percent of global energy production, and today it's nearly 23 percent of global energy production. Russia, the US and Canada combined produce about 46 percent of the world's natural gas.

Rest of the world
34.5%

Russia
22%

US
17.6%

Canada
6.4%

Turkmanistan
2.3%

Indonesia
2.4%

Netherlands
2.6%

UK
2.8%

Algeria
3.0%

Norway
3.1%

Islamic Rep of Iran
3.3%

China
6.5 million

Japan
5.4 million

Germany
and Russia
each with
2.6 million

Canada and
India each
with
2.3 million

Brazil
2.2 million

PETROLEUM MOVES THE WORLD
Petroleum products power virtually all motor vehicles, aircraft, marine vessels, and trains around the globe. In total, products derived from oil, such as motor gasoline, jet fuel, diesel fuel, and heating oil, supply nearly 40 percent of the energy consumed by households, businesses, and manufacturers worldwide. Natural gas and coal, by comparison, each supply less than 25 percent of the world's energy needs.

TOP CONSUMING NATIONS
The world consumes enough oil each year to fill a swimming pool 1 mile (1.6 km) square by one mile (1.6 km) deep. The US consumes more than 20 million barrels per day, a quarter of all the oil used in the world, and more than three times as much as its nearest rival, China. Most of the oil goes to fuel cars and trucks. China's energy consumption is accelerating. Although the number of cars in China doubled between 2000 and 2006, there remains one car for 40 people, compared with one car for every two people in the US. Dramatic additional vehicle growth in vehicle sales and demand for fuel are likely in China. The International Energy Agency forecasts that 60 percent of energy use could be in developing countries in 2030.

Saving oil

FOR MORE THAN A CENTURY, the world's oil consumption has risen nonstop, and demand is estimated to increase 60 percent over the next quarter century. Oil, natural gas and coal will continue to be the primary energy sources, with renewable energy sources and advanced technologies needed to meet rising energy demand. In addition, there are concerns about climate change. Both of these mean that we need to be careful about our consumption of energy by increasing energy efficiency. Energy efficiency is the cheapest and most plentiful form of new energy. Everybody can help our planet by making smart energy choices.

Aerodynamic shape reduces the energy needed to travel fast

TAKE THE TRAIN
Rather than travel in cars we could take trains, trams, and buses, which use two to three times less energy per person for every mile traveled than private cars. In cars more than in the US, under 5 percent of people travel to work on public transportation. Research has shown that if just 10 percent of Americans used public transportation regularly, the country's greenhouse gas emissions could be cut by over 25 percent.

DO SOME LEG WORK
The most environmentally friendly way of traveling is to walk or cycle. Many towns and cities have dedicated cycle lanes and paths to make cycling less hazardous and more enjoyable. Almost half of all the people in the UK admit to using a car or getting a lift for short trips that they could easily make on foot or by bicycle.

The human energy used to propel a bicycle is renewable and nonpolluting

"VAMPIRE" ENERGY
"Vampire energy" is a type of energy used by things that consume electricity 24 hours a day, even if you're not using them and they are turned off. These devices include televisions, VCRs and DVD players, computers, printers, stereos and microwaves. You can reduce your energy use by unplugging appliances directly from the wall when you're not using them. Be sure to turn off your computer if you're not using it.

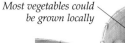

Most vegetables could be grown locally

Local produce is usually fresh, avoiding the need to use energy for refrigeration

SHOP LOCALLY
The food in a typical grocery cart has traveled thousands of miles to get there. So rather than drive to the supermarket and buy food transported from far away, we can save oil by shopping locally, especially at farmers' markets, where food comes directly from nearby farms.

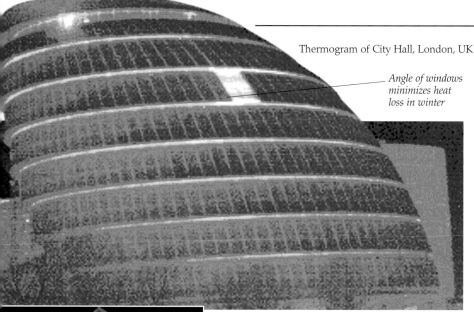

Thermogram of City Hall, London, UK

Angle of windows minimizes heat loss in winter

Most packaging can be recycled

About 40 million plastic bottles are thrown away each day in the USA

REDUCE HEAT LOSS

By recording how hot surfaces are, an infrared thermogram image can reveal heat loss from a building. The thermogram above shows that this old house loses most heat through the windows and roof (the white and yellow areas). This is why it is important to have storm windows and insulate roofs to block off the heat's escape routes. Many new buildings now incorporate energy-saving features. The construction, design, and unusual shape of London's City Hall (left) give it a cool exterior. It uses 75 percent less energy than a conventional building of the same size.

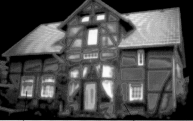

Windows let huge amounts of heat escape

Only thick walls cut heat loss to a minimum

RECYCLE WASTE

It almost always takes less energy to make things from recycled materials than from raw materials. Using scrap aluminum to make new soft drink cans, for example, uses 95 percent less energy than making the cans from raw aluminum ore. Unusually, it takes more energy to recycle plastic. However, it still saves oil because plastics mostly made from oil.

CUT ENERGY USE

We can save energy in the home by using less. Turning down the heating thermostat by just one degree saves a huge amount of energy. So does turning off unused lights, and switching off TVs and computers rather than keeping them on standby. Installing energy-saving fluorescent lightbulbs (right) can save even more, since they consume up to 80 percent less electricity than normal bulbs.

Energy-saving lightbulbs use less energy and last longer by staying cool

Succulent plants, such as sedum, are ideal for green roofs, since they tolerate water shortages and need little soil

GREEN ROOFS

In the future, more and more roofs could be "green" like this one, covered in living plants such as sedums and grasses—not just in the country, but in cities too. Chicago, for example, now has more than 250 office blocks with green roofs, and every new public building is given a green roof. Green roofs not only look attractive, but they also provide tremendous insulation, keeping the heat out in summer and holding it in during winter. This means that less energy is used for central heating and air-conditioning.

Oil substitutes

CONCERNS OVER THE WORLD'S increasing demands for energy and the effect of carbon dioxide emissions on the climate have encouraged people to look for different ways to power vehicles. Gasoline has a very high energy density and is easy to handle at room temperature and pressure, so it presents formidable competition to alternatives especially as a transportation fuel. Nearly all the major automakers are at work developing cars that use alternatives to oil, but most are still at the experimental stage. Some of the alternatives have few environmental benefits, and all have challenges to becoming economically feasible. It can take more than two decades for a newly commercialized technology to be broadly applied in the vehicle fleet on the road. Two examples are front-wheel drive and fuel injection technology. Improving fuel efficiency of cars is a solution to using less oil for transportation, and biomass, which converts crops and natural vegetation to energy sources is emerging as an option for transportation fuel.

FUEL FROM GARBAGE?
Every day, huge amounts of garbage are dumped in holes known as landfills. There bacteria break down materials such as food and paper, releasing a gas that is about 60 per cent methane. Scientists are trying to find ways to collect this methane and use it as a fuel.

WILDLIFE AT RISK
If extra land has to be plowed up to grow biofuel crops, wildlife may be put at risk. Intensive farming already makes it difficult for ground-nesting birds, including skylarks (above), to find suitable nesting sites, and insecticide use means that they struggle to find enough insects to feed their chicks.

Seeds contain high-energy oil

Flax

Corn contains carbohydrates that can be turned into ethanol

Corn

FUELS FROM PLANTS
Biofuels made from plants are renewable fuels, because we can grow more plants to replace the ones we use. Biofuels can be made by converting the sugar and starch in crops such as corn and sugar cane into ethanol, or by converting soybean, rapeseed, flaxseed, and other plant oils into biodiesel. Methanol can be produced from wood and farm waste. If every acre of corn in the US was used exclusively for ethanol production, less than 25 percent of the gasoline used could be replaced by ethanol. And biofuels are only a little cleaner than conventional fuels.

Rapeseed

Beans grow inside pods

Soybeans

HYDROGEN FROM METHANOL
One of the problems with cars powered by hydrogen fuel cells is that few gas stations have so far been adapted to supply hydrogen. So until hydrogen gas stations are widespread, hydrogen-powered cars will have to make their own hydrogen by extracting it from other fuels. Daimler-Chrysler's Necar 5 uses methanol as its hydrogen source. This can be supplied by pumps at conventional gas stations.

Daimler-Chrysler experimental Necar 5

Fuel cell is topped off with methanol from a cartridge

METHANOL PHONE
A cell phone battery must be recharged after a few hours of use. But scientists are developing tiny fuel cells that generate their own electricity to recharge the battery using methanol as a fuel. At present, most methanol is made from natural gas, since it is cheaper than making it from plant matter. So using methanol would not necessarily alter our reliance on fossil fuels.

BMW H2R

WATER AND SUNLIGHT
One day cars may be powered by hydrogen, either using fuel cells or, as in BMW's experimental H2R, a traditional internal combustion engine adapted to burn hydrogen instead of gasoline. A hydrogen car would produce no harmful exhaust gases. Hydrogen for filling the cars could be produced by using solar power to split water into hydrogen and oxygen. So the cars would effectively run on water and sunlight—the most renewable of all resources.

HOME REFINERY
Simple home units like this can convert vegetable oil into a diesel fuel called biodiesel, which burns slightly more cleanly than conventional diesel fuel. In warmer countries, biodiesel will run in ordinary diesel-engined vehicles. In cooler climates, it needs to be mixed in with conventional diesel.

KITCHEN POWER
A car engine can be altered to run on vegetable oil. The oil is obtained by crushing plants (straight vegetable oil, or SVO), or it can be waste vegetable oil from cooking (WVO). But the catering industry does not produce sufficient WVO to have much of an effect on gasoline consumption. And, as with biofuels, making SVO would require huge amounts of extra land to be given over to growing crops for fuel.

Inside the converter vegetable oil is thinned by mixing it with a substance called a lye

Biodiesel is drawn off from base of converter

Fuel for electricity

ABOUT 40% OF THE WORLD'S primary energy supply is used to generate electricity, and demand for electricity is accelerating in developing areas of the world. Power plants use a variety of fuels. Coal is the largest energy source used for generating electricity. Natural gas continues to grow in importance for electricity generation because it is cleaner burning than coal, and currently generates about 20% of the worlds electricity. Hydropower supplies 16% of the energy for power plants, while nuclear energy fuels about 15% of the world's electricity. Oil is primarily a transportation fuel, and only is used to generate about 7% of the world's electricity. All other sources, including geothermal, solar, wind, combustible renewables and wastes, generate only about 2% of electricity worldwide.

1. When swamp plants died their remains rotted slowly in stagnant water

2. Gradually, more and more remains piled up, squeezing lower layers dry and turning them into a soft mass called peat

3. Over millions of years, the peat was buried more than 2.5 miles (4 km) deep, where it began to cook in the heat of Earth's interior

4. Cooking destroyed the remaining plant fiber and drove out gases, leaving mainly solid black carbon

Layer or "seam" of coal

COAL

Coal is a non-renewable resource formed from layers of water and dirt that trapped dead plants at the bottom of swampy forests millions of years ago. The heat and pressure turned the plant remains into what we call coal. Coal is found on every continent, including Antarctica. Worldwide coal reserves are more than 1 trillion tons—enough to last approximately 180 years at current consumption levels. Coal may be burned directly for heat or cooking, but most is used in power plants to generate electricity. New technologies are significantly reducing the substantial greenhouse gases emitted by coal-burning power plants.

NUCLEAR

Nuclear energy is a non-renewable energy from the nucleus (core) of an atom. In nuclear fission, atoms split apart, releasing energy as heat. As the atom fragments hit other atoms, they also split, producing more heat. This heats water, which creates the steam that turns turbines to run generators that convert energy into electricity. Radioactive materials also diagnose and treat diseases, including cancer, remove dust from film and measure the amount of air whipped into ice cream! A single 6-g (1/3 oz) pellet of nuclear fuel yields as much energy as a ton of coal. Nuclear energy does not produce carbon dioxide—the major greenhouse gas—sulfur dioxide or nitrogen oxides. However, it creates dangerous radioactive waste, and heated wastewater from nuclear plants can harm aquatic life.

Hydrogen nucleus with two neutrons

Hydrogen nucleus with one neutron

Nuclei collide and fuse

Helium nucleus forms

Energy given out

Neutron released

GEOTHERMAL

Geothermal energy is generated in the earth's core about 4,000 miles below the surface. The continual slow decay of radioactive particles inside the earth creates temperatures hotter than the sun's surface. The hot rocks heat the water underground, which produces steam. Most geothermal reservoirs are found by drilling steam wells, with no visible clues above ground. However, they sometimes surface in volcanoes, hot springs and geysers. Most of the geothermal activity in the world occurs in an area that rims the Pacific Ocean called the Ring of Fire. Geothermal energy can heat homes and produce electricity by pumping the heated underground water or steam to the surface, with low emissions levels. Geothermal energy produces about 1/6 the carbon dioxide that a natural gas power plant emits. It is a renewable energy source because rainfall replenishes the water and the heat is continuously produced inside the earth.

WIND

Wind is a renewable resource and a form of solar energy. As hot air from the sun's radiation rises, the atmospheric pressure at the earth's surface declines, and cooler air replaces it resulting in wind. Wind turbines convert the wind's kinetic energy into mechanical power or electricity. They are not suitable for all locations because of the large space required and noise. However, wind farms (clusters of wind turbines) are making their mark in countries such as Denmark and Germany. We cannot predict when or how much the wind will blow, but it is a clean and inexhaustible source. And once wind turbines are built, it is inexpensive.

SOLAR

Solar energy is a renewable energy (light or heat) that comes from the sun. It can be converted directly or indirectly into other forms of energy, such as heat and electricity, without polluting the environment. Large areas are required to collect solar energy, and the initial investment is high. Solar panels made of steel, glass or plastic are used to capture heat from the sun, which then heats pipes carrying water or air. Photovoltaic (PV) cells convert heat from the sun directly into electricity. These can be used in a variety of ways, from providing power in hand-held devices, such as calculators, to generating electricity for an entire city.

WATER (HYDRO AND WAVE)

Waterpower has been used for thousands of years to grind corn and run simple machines. Today this renewable resource provides one-fifth of the world's electricity. Flowing water turns turbines to run generators that convert energy into electricity. Water is clean, reliable and powerful. It can be regulated to meet demand. However, it can be scarce during drought conditions and fossil fuels are often required for additional power. Dams or changes in water quality also can negatively impact aquatic habitats/terrestrial ecosystems. Waves caused by the wind blowing over the oceans' surface are also a tremendous source of energy. Waves can be bent into a narrow channel, increasing their power and size, which can be channeled into a catch basin or used directly to spin turbines. Waterpower systems are more expensive to operate than fossil fuel systems.

ENERGY, NOT OIL COMPANIES

Today's oil and gas companies are also today's energy companies, and are major investors in developing alternative energy sources. For example, BP is one of the world's largest producers of photovoltaic solar cells; Chevron is the world's largest developer of geothermal energy; the oil and gas industry is the largest producer and user of hydrogen; ExxonMobil, BP, Chevron, Shell, and ConocoPhillips are key players in government/industry hydrogen fuel and vehicle partnerships such as the US Department of Energy's FreedomCar and Fuel Partnership and the California Fuel Cell Partnership; and Shell is one of the top players in the worldwide wind industry.

World of job opportunities

Mᴏʀᴇ ᴛʜᴀɴ ᴏɴᴇ ᴍɪʟʟɪᴏɴ ᴘᴇᴏᴘʟᴇ are employed in the worldwide petroleum industry, and career opportunities are bright for those joining the industry. Careers range from manual fieldwork to skilled operators and maintenance technicians to professional engineering, science, and managerial positions. Exciting, challenging work is offered in variety of settings. Exploration field personnel and drilling workers frequently move from place to place. Well operation and natural gas processing workers usually stay in the same location for extended periods. Executives, administrators, and clerical workers generally work in office settings. Geologists, engineers, and managers may split their time between the office and jobsites, particularly during exploration work.

Photo: Woodside

Photo: Woodside

PROFESSIONALS

Geologist—Geologists study the composition, processes, and history of the Earth to find petroleum deposits. They can spend days to weeks charting, mapping, measuring, digging, and collecting samples of Earth. Then, in labs, they conduct tests to analyze what the samples are made of and how they evolved. Geologists use powerful computers to create and revise two- and three-dimensional models of the earth so they can make recommendations where to drill. A geologist applies knowledge of chemistry, physics, biology, and mathematics. Some entry-level geological jobs require only a bachelor's degree, but master's or doctoral degrees provide more opportunities for employment and advancement.

Petroleum Landman—A job unique to North America, petroleum landmen obtain permission from the landowner and acquire proper permits from various government agencies to drill a well. They are responsible for acquisition or disposition of oil, natural gas, or surface interests; negotiation, drafting, or management of agreements; and supervision of land administration activities. Most petroleum landman positions require a bachelor's degree in Petroleum Land Management. A Juris Doctorate (law) degree is greatly preferred for this job.

Geophysicist—A geophysicist studies the Earth using gravity, magnetic, electrical, and seismic methods. Some spend their time outdoors studying the Earth's features, while others stay indoors performing modeling calculations on computers. Geophysicists have a strong background in earth science with an emphasis on math, geology, and physics. A graduate degree is required for most geophysics jobs.

Petroleum Engineers—Involved in all phases of oil exploration, petroleum engineers search for oil and gas reservoirs, develop safe and efficient methods of bringing those resources to the Earth's surface, supervise site construction and operations, and contribute in taking down the oilrig after oil is extracted. Many petroleum engineers travel or live in other countries, taking them to deserts, high seas, mountains, and frigid regions to find untapped energy sources. Some work in offices, however, analyzing reports and recommendations of field engineers and advising corporate decision-makers on whether to proceed. Petroleum engineers must hold an undergraduate degree in engineering or earth science, and the majority of engineers continue their education to post-graduate degrees.

Photo: Shell Photographic Services, Shell International Ltd

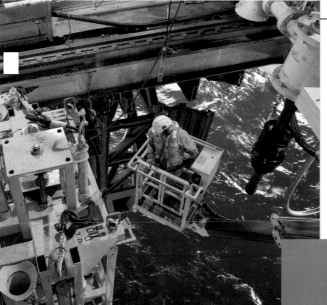

Photo: Transocean

Photo: BP

Photo: ©Norsk Hydro

"BIG CREW CHANGE"

The need for workers in the oil and gas industry is high now and could be higher in the coming years due to increased demand for oil and gas. The oil industry slump in the 1980s led to very little hiring and the number of students in geosciences education plummeted. Now the petroleum industry is booming and workers who transfer to other industries, retire, or leave the workforce provide a majority of job openings. The average age of the workforce is about 49, and these workers will need to be replaced in the coming 10 years. This means great opportunities to advance quickly.

SALARIES

The oil and gas industry offers the highest average industry salaries at every level than all other industries. Pay for the most physically demanding, entry-level oil jobs is even good. College-educated workers and technical school graduates in professional and technical occupations usually earn the most. Drillers' salaries vary by experience and training, and are generally a set day rate plus living allowance. Employees at offshore operations generally earn higher wages than workers at onshore oil fields because of more extreme working conditions.

Photo: BP

ENVIRONMENTAL/ SAFETY SPECIALISTS

Environmental Science and Protection Technicians—These technicians perform laboratory and field tests to monitor the environment and investigate sources of pollution. They may collect samples of gases, soil, water, and other materials for testing, and then take corrective actions as assigned.

Health and Safety Engineers—Applying knowledge of industrial processes, mechanics, chemistry, psychology, and industrial health and safety laws to promote worksite or product safety is the responsibility of health and safety engineers.

Photo: ©Norsk Hydro

Photo: BP

JOB REQUIREMENTS

Successful workers in the petroleum industry are typically mechanically inclined, safety conscious, good at following directions, and work well in a team. Workers can enter the industry with a variety of educational backgrounds. The most common entry-level field jobs, such as roustabouts or roughnecks, usually require little or no previous training or experience, but do require applicants to pass a physical examination. Basic skills are usually learned through on-the-job training. Advancement opportunities for oilfield workers are best for those with skill and experience. Offshore crews, even at the entry level, generally are more experienced than land crews because of the critical nature of the work. Professional jobs, such as geologist, geophysicist, or petroleum engineer, require at least a bachelor's degree, but many companies prefer a master's degree, and may require a Ph. D. Petroleum companies are actively seeking those with master's degrees.

REDUCING GAS FLARING

Crude oil and natural gas coexist under the earth, and drilling causes both resources to surface. Since capturing natural gas can be expensive and requires access to infrastructure for processing and transportation through pipelines, many crews flare (burn) the valuable gas. In Africa alone, flaring destroys 40 billion cubic meters of gas each year—enough to supply half of the electricity needed for the continent. The Global Gas Flaring Reduction Partnership to reduce flaring was formed by a coalition of oil companies and gas-producing countries, supported by the World Bank. The group has developed voluntary flaring and venting standards for its members that are helping countries to achieve their flaring reduction objectives more rapidly. The group also works to put natural and liquefied petroleum gas to use in local communities close to the flaring sites. There is more work to be done to reduce gas flaring, and the partnership has been extended to continue its efforts.

Serving society

ENERGY IS REQUIRED FOR EVERY activity we do—it provides heat for health and comfort, electricity for lighting and appliances, and power for vehicles. Sustainable energy means producing energy economically and safely in an environmentally and socially responsible manner that helps protect the well-being of future generations. Oil and gas companies often operate in less-developed regions and environmentally sensitive areas, and their operations may have a huge economic impact on the host countries. They have been pioneers in social responsibility in the communities where they operate by working with employees, their families, the local community, and society at-large to improve their quality of life, in ways that are both good for business and good for development. The examples of partnerships and projects provided here represent only a tiny portion of what the oil and gas industry is doing to build and maintain mutually beneficial relationships that serve society.

GETTING THE LEAD OUT

Air quality has greatly worsened in many developing countries due to urbanization and increased motor vehicle usage. Many cars continued to use leaded gasoline, although lead is a toxic compound and increases emissions that reduce air quality. More than 80 international organizations, including the Petroleum Industry of East Africa, came together to globally phase out leaded gasoline and adopt cleaner automotive technologies. Forming the Partnership for Clean Fuels and Vehicles, they began an educational campaign and implemented rules that have successfully phased out leaded gasoline in Sub-Saharan Africa. In early 2006, all production and importation of leaded gasoline ceased, and unleaded fuel became available to 100% of the population. PCFV continues to expand its efforts in other developing counties, such as Gambia and Thailand.

PROVIDING LOCAL DEVELOPMENT

When ConocoPhillips discovered oil reserves in the Gulf of Paria, an environmentally sensitive area off the coast of Venezuela, the local community voiced concerns regarding the impact production may have on the fishing industry, migratory birds, and the economy. ConocoPhillips assured them that it would protect the environment and give back to the community. The company has educated fishermen on preserving their catch, taught women profitable trade-skills, conducted health and wellness training, and increased access to drinking water. The company's local development program also includes hiring local workers, contributing to the continued growth of the economy, and working with conservation groups to preserve biological diversity.

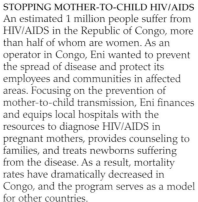

STOPPING MOTHER-TO-CHILD HIV/AIDS

An estimated 1 million people suffer from HIV/AIDS in the Republic of Congo, more than half of whom are women. As an operator in Congo, Eni wanted to prevent the spread of disease and protect its employees and communities in affected areas. Focusing on the prevention of mother-to-child transmission, Eni finances and equips local hospitals with the resources to diagnose HIV/AIDS in pregnant mothers, provides counseling to families, and treats newborns suffering from the disease. As a result, mortality rates have dramatically decreased in Congo, and the program serves as a model for other countries.

SAVE THE TIGER

In less than 100 years, the number of wild tigers dropped to fewer than 5,000, from the nearly 100,000 that once roamed Asia from Siberia to Sumatra. Trafficking of all tiger species was banned in 1987, but loss of habitat, poaching, and illegal trade of tiger skins still pose significant threats to the animals' continued survival. ExxonMobil first used the tiger's image to symbolize its products in the early 1900s. In 1995, the company formed the Save the Tiger Fund to support conservation of the world's remaining wild tigers. Through conservation education and advocacy, anti-poaching programs, habitat restoration and protection, and human-wildlife conflict resolution, ExxonMobil works with the local communities to restore the tiger population.

WORK SKILLS FOR PAKISTANI WOMEN

In the unindustrialized regions of southern Pakistan, the livelihood of many families depends on agriculture—an unreliable income source given the instability of the weather and inadequate irrigation systems. To provide for their families, men seek day labor in nearby cities, and women make crafts to sell at market. Women, however, lack the necessary training to fully develop their trade. BHP Billiton's Sartiyoon Silai Karhai Markaz Vocational Training Center encourages economic independence by teaching women to embroider, sew, and tailor. Hundreds have attended the center, and many women have even opened clothing and cosmetics shops in local villages.

TRAINING OF SHARIA JUDGES IN NIGERIA

Efforts to reform the political system in Nigeria led many northern states to implement Islamic law, called Sharia, and appoint religious leaders as judges. Although well versed in Islamic teachings and the Koran, many judges never receive formal legal education and lack the knowledge to apply human rights resolutions. Statoil, an integrated oil and gas company based in Norway, provided financial support to Nigeria's Legal Defence and Assistance Project (LEDAP), which allowed the group to conduct human rights training seminars for 20 percent of the judges in the country.

Timeline

FOR THOUSANDS OF YEARS, especially in the Middle East, oil was used for a variety of purposes, from burning in lamps to waterproofing roofs and making ships leakproof. However, the global oil age only really began about 150 years ago. The turning points were the introduction of the first kerosene lamps in 1857 and, more importantly, the invention of the internal combustion engine in 1862, which led to the development of the automobile. Today, oil not only supports the world economy, but it is also a major influence in world politics.

Zoroastrian fire temple in Azerbaijan

Egyptian mummy case

C. 4500 BCE
People in what is now Iraq use bitumen from natural oil seeps to waterproof their houses.

C. 4000 BCE
People in the Middle East use bitumen to seal boats against leaks. This is called caulking, and it continues until the 1900s.

C. 600 BCE
King Nebuchadnezzar uses bricks containing bitumen to build the Hanging Gardens of Babylon, and bitumen-lined pipes to supply the gardens with water.

500S BCE
Persian archers put bitumen on their arrows to turn them into flaming missiles.

450 BCE
The Ancient Greek historian Herodotus describes bitumen pits near Babylon, which are highly valued by the Babylonians.

C. 300 BCE
Followers of the Zoroastrian religion build fire temples in places such as Azerbaijan. Natural gas from underground is used to fuel a constantly burning flame within the temple.

C. 200 BCE
The Ancient Egyptians sometimes use bitumen when mummifying their dead.

C. 1 BCE
The Chinese extract oil and gas when drilling for salt. They burn the gas to dry out the salt.

CE 67
Jews defending the city of Jotapata use boiling oil against Roman attackers.

100
The Roman historian Plutarch describes oil bubbling up from the ground near Kirkuk (in present day Iraq). This is one of the first historical records of liquid oil.

500S
Byzantine ships use "Greek fire" bombs made with bitumen, sulfur, and quicklime.

1264
The Venetian merchant and adventurer Marco Polo records seeing oil from seeps near Baku (in present day Azerbaijan) being collected in large quantities for use in medicine and lighting.

1500s
In Krosno, Poland, oil from seeps in the Carpathian Mountains is burned in street lamps.

1780s
Swiss physicist Aimé Argand's whale-oil lamp supersedes all other types of lamp.

C. 1800
Tarmacadam (a mixture of graded gravel and tar) is first used to provide a good road surface.

1807
Coal gas provides the fuel for the world's first real street lights in London, England.

1816
Start of the US coal gas industry in Baltimore.

1821
Natural gas is first supplied commercially in Fredonia, New York, with gas being piped through hollow logs to houses.

1846
Canadian Abraham Gesner makes kerosene from coal.

1847
The world's first oil well is drilled at Baku, Azerbaijan.

1849
Abraham Gesner discovers how to make kerosene from crude oil.

1851
In Canada, Charles Nelson Tripp and others form North America's first oil company, the International Mining and Manufacturing Company, to extract asphalt from tar beds in Ontario.

1851
Scottish chemist James Young opens the world's first oil refinery at Bathgate, near Edinburgh, Scotland, to produce oil from the rock torbanite, a type of oil shale.

Kerosene lamp

1853
Polish chemist Ignacy Lukasiewiz discovers how to make kerosene from crude oil on an industrial scale. This paves the way for the kerosene lamp, which will revolutionize home lighting later in the decade.

1856
Ignacy Lukasiewiz sets up the world's first crude oil refinery at Ulaszowice in Poland.

1857
American Michael Dietz patents a clean-burning lamp designed to burn kerosene, rather than the more expensive whale oil. Within a few years, kerosene lamps will force whale-oil lamps off the market.

1858
North America's first oil well opens at Oil Springs, Ontario, in Canada.

1859
The US's first oil well is drilled by Edwin L. Drake at Titusville, Pennsylvania.

1860
The Canadian Oil Company becomes the world's first integrated oil company, controlling production, refining, and marketing.

1861
Oil carried aboard the sailing ship *Elizabeth Watts* from Pennsylvania to London is the first recorded shipping of oil.

J. D.
Rockefeller

1862
Frenchman Alphonse Beau de Rochas patents the four-stroke internal combustion engine. Fueled by gas, it will power most cars in the 20th century.

1863
American businessman J. D. Rockefeller starts an oil refining company in Cleveland, Ohio.

1870
J. D. Rockefeller forms Standard Oil (Ohio), later known as Esso, and today as ExxonMobil.

1872
J. D. Rockefeller takes over 25 percent of the US petroleum market. By 1877 he will control about 90 percent of all oil refining in the US.

1878
The first oil well in Venezuela is set up at Lake Maracaibo.

1879
American Thomas Edison invents the electric lightbulb.

1885
In Germany, engineer and industrialist Gottlieb Daimler invents the first modern-style gas engine, using an upright cylinder and a carburetor to feed in the petrol.

1885
German engineer Karl Benz creates the world's first practical gas-engined car for general sale.

1885
Oil is discovered in Sumatra by the Royal Dutch oil company.

1891
The Daimler Motor Company begins producing gasoline engines in the US for tram cars, carriages, quadricycles, fire engines, and boats.

1901
The US's first deep-oil well and gusher at Spindletop, Texas, trigger the Texas oil boom.

Ford Model T

1905
The Baku oil field is set on fire during unrest throughout the Russian Empire against the rule of Czar Nicholas II.

1907
The British oil company Shell and Royal Dutch merge to form Royal Dutch Shell.

1908
The first mass-produced car, the Model T Ford, is launched. As mass-production makes cars affordable to ordinary people, car ownership rises rapidly and demand for gasoline soars.

1908
Oil is found in Persia (modern Iran), leading to the formation of the Anglo-Persian Oil company—the forerunner of the modern oil giant BP—in 1909.

1910
The first oil discovery in Mexico is made at Tampico on the Gulf Coast.

1914–18
During World War I, British control of the Persian oil supply for ships and planes is a crucial factor in the defeat of Germany.

1932
Oil is discovered in Bahrain.

1935
Nylon is invented, one of the first synthetic fabrics made from oil products.

1935
Cat cracking is first used in oil refining. This uses intense heat and a substance called a catalyst to split up heavy hydrocarbons.

1938
Major oil reserves are discovered in Kuwait and Saudi Arabia.

1939–45
World War II: the control of oil supplies, especially from Baku and the Middle East, plays a key role in the Allied victory.

1948
The world's largest liquid oil field is discovered in Ghawar, Saudi Arabia, holding about 80 billion barrels.

1951
The Anglo Persian (now Iranian) Oil Company is nationalized by the Iranian government, leading to a coup backed by the US and Britain to restore the power of the Shah (king).

Timeline continues on page 70

Nylon rope

The Trans-Alaska pipeline

1960
OPEC (Organization of Petroleum Exporting Countries) is founded by Saudi Arabia, Venezuela, Kuwait, Iraq, and Iran.

1967
Commercial production of oil begins at the Alberta tar sands in Canada, the world's largest oil resource.

1968
Oil is found at Prudhoe Bay, northern Alaska. This becomes North America's major source of oil.

1969
In the US, a vast oil spill started by a blow-out at a rig off the coast of Santa Barbara, California, damages marine life.

1969
Oil and natural gas are discovered in the North Sea, leading to a 25-year energy bonus for countries such as the UK.

1971
OPEC countries in the Middle East begin to nationalize their oil assets to regain control over their reserves.

1973
OPEC quadruples oil prices. It halts supplies to Western countries supporting Israel in its war against Arab forces led by Egypt and Syria. This causes severe oil shortages in the West.

1975
Oil production begins at North Sea oil rigs.

1975
In response to the 1973 oil crisis, the Strategic Petroleum Reserve (SPR) is set up in the US to build up an emergency supply of oil in salt domes. By 2005, the US will have 658 million barrels of oil stored in this way.

1977
The Trans-Alaska oil pipeline is completed.

1979
Three-Mile Island nuclear power plant incident occurs in Harrisburg, Pennsylvania, with some radioactive material released.

1979–81
Oil prices rise from US $13.00 to $34.00 per barrel.

Cleaning up after the *Exxon Valdez* oil spill

1989
The tanker *Exxon Valdez* runs aground in Prince William Sound, Alaska, causing an environmental catastrophe as oil spills on to the Alaskan coast.

1991
Kuwaiti oilfields are set alight in the Gulf War.

1995
A UN resolution allows a partial resumption of Iraqi oil exports in the "oil for food" deal.

1996
Qatar opens the world's first major liquid natural gas (LNG) exporting facility.

2002
Construction on the BTU pipeline from Baku to the Mediterranean begins.

2003
The US Senate rejects a proposal to allow oil exploration in the Arctic National Wildlife Refuge (ANWR) in northern Alaska.

2003
The first US delivery of liquefied natural gas (LNG) since 1980 is made to the reactivated Cove Point LNG regasification plant in Maryland, which will be the largest LNG regastification facility in the United States.

A flooded oil installation in the US hit by Hurricane Katrina in 2005

2004
US oil imports hit a record 11.3 million million barrels per day.

2004
North Sea production of oil and gas declines.

2005
Hurricane Katrina strikes the Gulf Coast, causing chaos in the US oil industry.

2005
The price of oil reaches US $70.80 per barrel.

2006
Russia stops gas supplies to Ukraine until the Ukranians agree to pay huge price rises.

2006
BP partially shuts down the Prudhoe Bay oil field due to corrosion of its Alaskan pipeline.

2006
Chevron's Jack 2 deepwater discovery in the Gulf of Mexico is believed to be the biggest discovery in the United States since the discovery of Prudhoe Bay.

2007
The International Energy Agency projects that China will overtake the US as the world's biggest carbon dioxide emitter in 2007, and India will be the third-largest emitter by 2015.

MUSEUM TRIPS

Many science and natural history museums have excellent exhibits covering topics raised in this book, including energy resources, fossil fuel formation, transport, and so on. If you are lucky, you may live near a specialist museum, such as the US's Drake Well Museum in Titusville, Pennsylvania, and the California Oil Museum in Santa Paula, or the UK's National Gas Museum in Leicester.

Find out more

THIS BOOK HAS GIVEN a taster of the world's largest and most complex industry, but your voyage of discovery need not end here. You can find out more about the geology of oil by exploring the rocks in your area and learning to identify the sedimentary rocks in which oil forms. You can also find out about the history, science, and technology of oil by visiting museums. Energy websites can tell you more about making smart energy choices.

Museum model of an offshore rig

VISITS AND VIRTUAL TOURS

Your school may be able to arrange a visit to an oil refinery or terminal, or to a filling station. The education departments of major oil companies can usually advise where this is possible. But oil installations are often sited in remote locations, and the processes that take place there may be too dangerous to make school visits possible, so virtual tours may be a better option. The Institute of Petroleum and ExxonMobil have set up virtual tours of the UK's Fawley oil refinery and the Captain oil rig in the North Sea. See the links in the Useful Websites box above.

Waste materials for recycling

Recycling can reduce our energy consumption

Panoramas and detailed views help to explain the refining process

Virtual tour of an oil refinery

USEFUL WEBSITES

- Information about all energy sources and E&P industry careers: **http://www.energy4me.org**, presented by the Society of Petroleum Engineers
- A list of specialist oil and gas museums around the world: **http://www.energy4me.org/oilgas/museums.htm**
- Virtual tour of the Fawley oil refinery, UK: **http://resources.schoolscience.co.uk/Exxonmobil/index.html**
- A child's visit to an offshore oil rig: **www.mms.gov/mmskids/explore/explore.htm**
- A young person's guide to oil and gas, Institute of Petroleum: **http://www.energyinst.org.uk/education/ypg/ypg4.htm**
- Students' page from the Society of Exploration Geophysics: **http://students.seg.org/K12/kids.htm**
- Facts, games, and activities about energy, plus links: **www.eia.doe.gov/kids/index.html**
- A US Department of Energy site about fossil fuels, including coal, oil, and natural gas: **www.fe.doe.gov/education/energylessons/index.html**
- A comprehensive guide to oil refining: **http://science.howstuffworks.com/oil-refining.htm**
- The Chevron company's Learning Centre, packed with facts: **www.chevron.com/products/learning_center/**
- Basic geology, how oil forms, and how it is found: **www.priweb.org/ed/pgws/index.html**
- All about fuel cells, from the Smithsonian Institute: **http://americanhistory.si.edu/fuelcells/**
- An introduction to nuclear power from the US's Nuclear Energy Institute: **www.nei.org/scienceclub/index.html**
- The Alliance to Save Energy's kids site: **www.ase.org/section/_audience/consumers/kids**
- Plenty of links on the topic "Recycle, Reduce, Reuse": **http://42explore.com/recycle.htm**
- The US's National Institute of Environmental Health Sciences site on recycling and reducing waste: **www.niehs.nih.gov/kids/recycle.htm**

Index

Acknowledgments

Dorling Kindersley would like to thank: Hilary Bird for the index; Dawn Bates for proofreading; Claire Bowers, David Ekholm-JAlbum, Clarie Ellerton, Sunita Gahir, Joanne Little, Susan St Louis, Steve Setford, & Bulent Yusef for help with the clip art; David Ball, Kathy Fahey, Neville Graham, Rose Horridge, Joanne Little, & Sue Nicholson for the wall chart; and Margaret Parrish for Americanization work on the original edition of this title; Dorling Kindersley would like to thank Margaret Watson (SPE); Kelly D. Maish for her redesign and composition work; Heather MacNeil for the index; Katherine Linder for image manipulation; and Karen Whitehouse for their editorial work on the custom .

The publisher would also like to thank the following for their kind permission to reproduce their photographs:

a-above; b-below/bottom; c-center; f-far; l-left; r-right; t-top

The Advertising Archives: 15tr, 15bc; akg-images: 12cl; Alamy Images: AGStockUSA, Inc. 39tc; Bryan & Cherry Alexander Photography 20–21b, 35b; allOver Photography 53br; Roger Bamber 37cra; G.P. Bowater 34tl, 39tr; Nick Cobbing 50tl; Richard Cooke 52l; John Crall / Transtock Inc. 15l; CuboImages srl 21cr; Patrick Eden 60–61c; Paul Felix Photography 23br; The Flight Collection 49tr; David R. Frazier Photolibrary, Inc. 54tl; Paul Glendell 56ftr; Robert Harding Picture Library Ltd 51t; imagebroker / Stefan Obermeier 45br; ImageState 50ca; Andre Jenny 52br; kolvenbach 41cl; Lebrecht Music and Arts Photo Library 11bl; Kari Marttila 45cl; Gunter Marx 70br; North Wind Picture Archive 11br; Phototake Inc. 19cra; Popperfoto 9c; Patrick Steel 48bc; Stock Connection Blue 36–37c; Angel Svo 21tc; Visual Arts Library (London) 8b; mark wagner aviation-images 41b; Worldspec / NASA 7tr; Courtesy of Apple. Apple and the Apple logo are trademarks of Apple Computer Inc., registered in the US and other countries: 6c, 69br (Laptop); The Art Archive: 8tr; Bibliothèque des Arts Décoratifs Paris / Dagli Orti 61cra; Biodys Engineering: 55tr; Courtesy of BMW: 55b; Provided by BP p. l.c.: 47crb, 47br, 64–65 (Background), 66–67 (Background), 68tl, 68–69 (Background), 69br (On Screen), 70–71 (Background); The Bridgeman Art Library: Private Collection, Archives Charmet 9tl; Corbis: 27tr; Bettmann 12tc, 12tr, 14cl, 48c, 67bl; Jamil Bittar / Reuters 51bl; Lloyd Cluff 35tr; Corbis Sygma 49cra; Eye Ubiquitous / Mike Southern 59tr; Natalie Fobes 68c; Lowell Georgia 31tr; Martin Harvey / Gallo Images 37bc; Hulton-Deutsch Collection 21tl; Hulton-Deutsch Collection 14bl, 15cr; Langevin Jacques / Corbis Sygma 35cra; Ed Kashi 47bl; Karen Kasmauski 37br; Matthias Kulka 65t; Lake County Museum 40tl; Jacques Langevin / Corbis Sygma 46c; Lester Lefkowitz 6–7bc; Stephanie Maze 33cl; Francesc Muntada 62–63b; Kazuyoshi Nomachi 39b; Stefanie Pilick / dpa 23t; Jose Fuste Raga 46b; Roger Ressmeyer 38tl, 40cl, 63tl; Reuters 32tc; Otto Rogge 58b; Bob Rowan / Progressive Image 29c; Grafton Marshall Smith 58cr; Lara Solt / Dallas Morning News 26tl; Paul A. Souders 61tr; Stocktrek 63tr; Ted Streshinsky 35tl; Derek Trask 6bl; Peter Turnley 48–49c; Underwood & Underwood 13br; Tim Wright 29c; DaimlerChrysler AG: 55tc; DK Images: The British Museum 9cl, 66bl; Simon Clay / Courtesy of the National Motor Museum, Beaulieu 14tl; Tim Draper / Rough Guides 19tl; Neil Fletcher / Oxford University Museum of Natural History 2bl, 23bl; Peter Hayman / The British Museum 9tr; Chas Howson / The British Museum 9crb; Jon Hughes / Bedrock Studios 22tc; Judith Miller / Ancient Art 2cra, 11tl; Colin Keates / Courtesy of the Natural History Museum, London 3tl, 16cl, 25tr (Sandstone), 27tl, 33bl, 70tl; Dave King / Courtesy of the National Motor Museum, Beaulieu 14c; Dave King / Courtesy of The Science Museum, London 10cl, 11tr; Judith Miller / Cooper Owen 9fcl; Judith Miller / Luna 44c; Judith Miller / Toy Road Antiques 23cr; Judith Miller / Wallis & Wallis 44tl; NASA 50bl; James Stevenson & Tina Chambers / National Maritime Museum, London 4tc, 21cl; Clive Streeter / Courtesy of The Science Museum, London 4cl, 10–11c, 56tr; Linda Whitwam / Courtesy of the Yufuin Folk Art Museum, Japan 60cl; Photograph Courtesy of EFDA-JET: 63cr; Empics Ltd: EPA 45tl; Getty Images: AFP 61crb; Alexander Drozdov / AFP 20cl; Jerry Grayson / Helifilms Australia PTY Ltd. 68br; Paul S. Howell / Liaison 31tr; Hulton Archive 27crb, 48tl; Image Bank / Cousteau Society 33br; Alex Livesey 47tc; Lonely Planet Images / Jim Wark 41bl; Jamie McDonald 47tr; Carl Mydans / Time Life Pictures 48cla; National Geographic / Justin Guariglia 32cl; National Geographic / Sarah Leen 16tl; Mustafa Ozer / AFP 34br; Photographer's Choice / David Seed Photography 57tr; Photographer's Choice / Joe McBride 7tl; Photographer's Choice / Rich LaSalle 71tl; Stone / David Frazier 56–57c; Stone / David Hiser 23cl; Stone / Keith Wood 37tc; Stone / Tom Bean 50crb; Stone + / Tim Macpherson 6tr; Sergei Supinsky / AFP 49c; Texas Energy Museum / Newsmakers 13tr; Three Lions 13tl; Yoshikazu Tsuno / AFP 55cl; Greg Wood / AFP 45tr; Landsat 7 satellite image courtesy of NASA Landsat Project Science Office and USGS National Center for Earth Resources Observation Science: 25tl; Library Of Congress, Washington, D.C.: 13c; F.J. Frost, Port Arthur, Texas 30tl; Warren K. Leffler 48bl; Magenn Power Inc. (www.magenn.com): Chris Radisch 57br; Mary Evans Picture Library: 10tr, 20tl, 46tl; Micro-g Lacoste: 29cr; NASA: 59bl; Dryden Flight Research Center Photo Collection 59c; JPL 34bl; Jeff Schmaltz, MODIS Rapid Response Team, GSFC 18cr; National Geographic Image Collection: 42–43b; The Natural History Museum, London: 25bc, 25br; Michael Long 27cla; Oil Museum of Canada, Oil Springs, Ontario: 12bl; Rex Features: Norm Betts 26cl, 26–27b; SIPA Press 61bc; ROSEN Swiss AG: 34c; Science & Society Picture Library: 27c, 45cl; Science Photo Library: Eye of Science 43tc; Ken M. Johns 25c; Laguna Design 16–17c; Lawrence Livermore Laboratory 63ca; Tony McConnell 53cl; Carlos Munoz-Yague / Eurelios 51br; Alfred Pasieka 53cr; Paul Rapson 6tl, 17br, 39tl; Chris Sattlberger 28cl; Still Pictures: Joerg Boethling 54bl; Mark Edwards 12–13bc; Russell Gordon 30cr; Walter H. Hodge 24–25b; Knut Mueller 66tr; Darlyne A. Murawski 18b; S.Compoint / UNEP 31b; TopFoto.co.uk: HIP / The British Library 9br; Dr Richard Tyson, School of Geoscience and Civil Engineering, Newcastle University: 19clb; © TOTAL UK Limited 2005: 64cr; Vattenfall Group: 56cr; Auke Visser, Holland: 36cb; Wikipedia, The Free Encyclopedia: 2cl, 44tr; Woodside Energy Ltd. (www.woodside.com.au): 5tr, 28cr, 28bl, 29b.

NEW IMAGES FOR CUSTOM SPE-EDITION: Petrobras: 28; US National Energy Technology Laboratory: 22; Anadarko Petroleum Corporation: 23; Canadian Society for Unconventional Gas: 23; Petro-Canada: 30; Saudi Aramco: 36; BP: 36; © Norsk Hydro: 37; Shell: 64; Woodside: 64; Transocean: 65; © Norsk Hydro: 65; BP: 65.

Jacket images: Front: Alamy Images: Popperfoto tl; Corbis: Reuters tr; Getty Images: Gandee Vasan b; Science Photo Library: Paul Rapson tc. Back: Alamy Images: Justin Kase cra; Getty Images; Science Photo Library: Laguna Design Paul Rapson tr; Still Pictures: Alfred Pasieka S.Compoint/UNEP br.

All other images © Dorling Kindersley
For further information see: www.dkimages.com